GERMAN

PHRASE BOOK
AND
DICTIONARY

by Charles A. Hughes

GROSSET & DUNLAP, INC.
A National General Company

New York

Published simultaneously in Canada

Library of Congress Catalog Card No.: 71-144061
ISBN: 0-448-00652-9
Printed in the U.S.A.

CONTENTS

INTRODUCTION

In this phrase book for travel in the German-speaking countries, we have tried to incorporate features that will make it convenient and easy for you to use in actual situations. Every phrase and word is translated into proper German and then respelled to guide you in its pronunciation.

The book is also "programmed" to help you with two of the basic problems of the novice in a language — an inability to comprehend the spoken word and a certain hesitancy in speaking out. To solve the first problem, questions have been avoided, to the extent possible, in the phrases. When they could not be avoided, they have been worded so that a yes or no answer may be expected. And sometimes, when even this solution is impossible, the anticipated answer is given. To solve the problem of hesitancy, the contents of the book have been arranged so that a minimal command of the basic phrases, salutations, weather, numbers, time, statements of need and desire, may be acquired in the first sections. The pronunciation guides printed under the German translations should also give you confidence that you will be understood. If your listener should indicate that he doesn't understand, merely try again. A slight mispronunciation is no embarrassment.

Finally, to aid you in finding a phrase that you wish to use, the Dictionary has been partially indexed. The Dictionary itself is comprehensive enough so that you should not lack for words.

TIPS ON PRONUNCIATION AND ACCENT

The pronunciation of each word in this phrase book is indicated by a respelling that approximates the sounds of German, according to the following system:

The vowels:

ah	Pronounced like "a" in f*a*ther
eh	Pronounced like "e" in th*ey*
e	Pronounced like "e" in m*e*t
ee	Pronounced like "ee" in s*ee*n
i	Pronounced like "i" in p*i*n
ī	Pronounced like the pronoun *I* or the word *eye*
oh	Pronounced like "o" in *o*ver
o	Pronounced like "o" in b*o*y
o͡e	Pronounced like "u" in f*u*r (but with pursed lips)
oo	Pronounced like "oo" in f*oo*d
e͡u	Pronounced like "i" in mach*i*ne (but with pursed lips)
ow	Pronounced like "ow" in n*ow*
oy	Pronounced like "oy" in b*oy*

In a final unaccented syllable, the "e" in the combinations "-el," "-em," "-en," and "-es" is pronounced very short, somewhat like the final "e" in hous*e*s or the final "e" in fath*e*r. This sound is indicated by an ordinary "e" in the transcriptions.

All vowels in German may be pronounced either long or short. In the written language, long vowels are indicated by doubling the vowel or by placing an "h" after the vowel.

Consonants are sounded approximately as in English, with these exceptions:

"ch"	in the written language has two sounds. The first, like "h" in *h*ole, but sounded farther back in the throat, follows a back vowel (a, o, u). It is transcribed here as "kh." The second, pronounced like "h" in *h*iss, in the front of the mouth, follows front vowels (e, i, ä, ö, ü). It is transcribed here as "c."
"g"	in final position has the same two sounds as "ch" described above.
"j"	is always pronounced like "y" in *y*ou.

"s"	at the beginning of a word sounds like a light "z" in *z*ebra.
"ss"	sounds like "ss" in mi*ss*.
"sch"	and "s" before "p" and "t" are sounded like "sh" in *sh*oe.
"v"	is pronounced like "f" in *f*irst.
"w"	is pronounced like "v" in *v*ery.
"z"	is pronounced like "ts" in ca*ts*.

In the pronunciations the stress or main accent in a word is indicated by an accent mark (') after the stressed syllable.

eye	opportunity,
Auge	Gelegenheit
ow'-ge	*ge-leh'-gen-hīt*

Salutations and Greetings

Even before you learn anything else in a foreign language, you will want to learn how to greet people. Here are some short expressions that you will find easy to learn and to use when you meet people in a foreign land or along the way, perhaps on the ship or the plane.

Good morning.
Guten Morgen.
Goot'-en mor'-gen.

Good day.
Guten Tag.
Goot'-en tahkh.

Good afternoon.
Guten Tag.
Goot'-en tahkh.

Good evening.
Guten Abend.
Goot'-en ah'-bent.

Good bye.
Leben Sie wohl.
Leh'-ben zee vohl.

Good night.
Gute Nacht.
Goot'-e nahkht.

How are you?
Wie geht es Ihnen?
Vee geht es ee'-nen?

Well, thank you. And you?
Gut, danke. Und Ihnen?
Goot, dahnk'-e. Unt ee'-nen?

How is Mr. . . . ?
Wie geht es dem Herrn . . . ?
Vee geht es dehm hern . . . ?

How is Mrs. . . . ?
Wie geht es der Frau . . . ?
Vee geht es dehr frow . . . ?

Is Miss . . . well?
Geht es dem Fraülein . . . gut?
Geht es dehm froy'-lin . . . goot?

May I present my wife?
Darf ich meine Frau vorstellen?
Dahrf iç mi'-ne frow for'-shtel-en?

This is my husband.
Dies is mein Mann.
Dees ist min mahn.

Pleased to meet you.
Sehr erfreut. Sehr angenehm.
Zehr ehr-froyt'. Zehr ahn'-ge-nehm.

This is my friend. (m)
Dies ist mein Freund.
Dees ist min froynt.

This is my friend. (f)
Dies ist meine Freundin.
Dees ist mi'-ne froyn'-din.

This is my mother and my father.
Dies ist meine Mutter und mein Vater.
Dees ist mi'-ne mu'-ter unt min fah'-ter.

This is my sister and my brother.
Dies ist meine Schwester und mein Bruder.
Dees ist mi'-ne shves'-ter unt min broo'-der.

Is this your daughter?
Ist das Ihre Tochter?
Ist dahs ee'-re tokh'-ter?

Is this your son?
Ist das Ihr Sohn?
Ist dahs eer zohn?

I hope that we will meet again.
Ich hoffe, wir werden uns wiedersehen.
Iç hof'-e, veer ver'-den uns vee'-der-zeh-en.

I'll see you tomorrow.
Ich werde Sie morgen sehen.
Iç ver'-de zee mor'-gen zeh'-en.

I'll be seeing you.
Auf Wiedersehen.
Owf vee'-der-zeh-en.

Excuse me.
Entschuldigen Sie mich.
Ent-shul'-dee-gen zee miç.

Pardon me.
Verzeihen Sie mir. / Verzeihung.
Fer-tsī-en zee meer. / Fer-tsī'-ung.

I'm very sorry.
Es tut mir leid.
Es toot meer līt.

You're welcome.
Bitte schön.
Bit'-e shœn.

Please.
Bitte.
Bit'-e.

Don't mention it.
Es ist nichts.
Es ist niçts.

With pleasure.
Mit Vergnügen.
Mit ferg-neūg'-en.

Good luck!
Viel Glück!
Feel gleūk!

The Weather

The weather is one thing everyone has in common, and it is a universal topic of conversation. The phrases given here — combined with a bit of added vocabulary — are easily mastered, for they "pattern" in an understandable manner: "It's raining." "It's snowing."

It's nice weather today.
Es ist heute schönes Wetter.
Es ist hoy'-te shöen'-es vet'-er.

It's bad weather today.
Es ist heute schlechtes Wetter.
Es ist hoy'-te shleçt'-es vet'-er.

It's cold.
Es ist kalt.
Es ist kahlt.

It's warm.
Es ist warm.
Es ist vahrm.

Is it raining?
Regnet es?
Rehg'-net es?

Yes, it's raining.
Ja, es regnet.
Yah, es rehg'-net.

No, it's not raining.
Nein, es regnet nicht.
Nin, es rehg'-net niçt.

It's snowing.
Es schneit.
Es shnīt.

It rains (snows) here every day.
Es regnet (schneit) jeden Tag hier.
Es rehg'-net (shnīt) yeh'-den tahkh heer.

It's beginning to rain (to snow).
Es fängt an zu regnen (zu schneien).
Es fengt ahn tsoo rehg'-nen (tsoo shnī'-en).

It often rains (snows) here.
Es regnet (schneit) oft hier.
Es rehg'-net (shnīt) oft heer.

It will rain (snow) tomorrow.
Es wird morgen regnen (schneien).
Es veert mor'-gen rehg'-nen (shnī'-en).

It rained (snowed) yesterday.
Es hat gestern geregnet (geschneit).
Es haht ges'-tern ge-rehg'-net (ge-shnīt').

It has stopped raining (snowing).
Es hat aufgehört zu regnen (schneien).
Es haht owf'-ge-höert tsoo rehg'-nen (shnī'-en).

It's windy.
Es ist windig.
Es ist vin'-deeç.

There's a lot of fog.
Es gibt viel Nebel.
Es geept feel neh'-bel.

The sun is rising.
Die Sonne geht auf.
Dee zon'-e geht owf.

The sun is setting.
Die Sonne geht unter.
Dee zon'-e geht un'-ter.

How is the weather?
Wie ist das Wetter?
Vee ist dahs vet'-er?

I need an umbrella.
Ich brauche einen Regenschirm.
Iç brow'-khe in'-en rehg'-en-sheerm.

Will it be cool there?
Wird es dort kühl sein?
Veert es dort kēul zin?

Will it be damp there?
Wird es dort feucht sein?
Veert es dort foyçt zin?

Should I take a sweater?
Sollte ich eine Wolljacke mitnehmen?
Zol'-te iç i'-ne vol'-yah-ke mit'-neh-men?

a raincoat?
einen Regenmantel?
i'-nen rehg'-en-mahn-tel?

a jacket?
eine Jacke?
i'-nen yah'-ke?

It's lightning.
Es blitzt.
Es blitst.

It's thundering.
Es donnert.
Es don'-ert.

Cold weather.
Kaltes Wetter.
Kahlt'-es vet'-er.

Warm weather.
Warmes Wetter.
Vahrm'-es vet'-er.

Cold water.
Kaltes Wasser.
Kahlt'-es vahs'-er.

Warm water.
Warmes Wasser.
Vahrm'-es vahs'-er.

Hot water.
Heisses Wasser.
His'-es vahs'-er.

I see . . .	I like . . .	I'm afraid of . . .
Ich sehe . . .	Ich habe . . . gern	Ich fürchte . . .
Iç zeh'-e . . .	*Iç hah'-be . . . gehrn*	*Iç fẽůrç'-te . . .*

the rain.	the wind.	the snow.
den Regen.	den Wind.	den Schnee.
dehn rehg'-en.	*den vint.*	*dehn shneh.*

the ice.	the sky.	the sun.
das Eis.	den Himmel.	die Sonne.
dahs is.	*dehn him'-el.*	*dee zon'-e.*

the moon.	the stars.	a star.
den Mond.	die Sterne.	einen Stern.
dehn mont.	*dee shter'-ne.*	*i'-nen shtern.*

a rainbow.	a cloud.	the clouds.
einen Regenbogen.	eine Wolke.	die Wolken.
i'-nen rehg'-en-boh-gen.	*i'-ne vol'-ke.*	*dee vol'-ken.*

the lightning.	the thunder.
den Blitz.	den Donner.
dehn blits.	*dehn don'-er.*

the storm.
den Sturm. / das Gewitter.
dehn stoorm. / dahs ge-vit'-er.

General Expressions

In this section you will find the most useful expressions — the ones you will use over and over again. They are the phrases that you should have on the tip of the tongue, ready for immediate use — particularly those that express desire or volition. Here they have been kept short for easy acquisition and speedy communication. You will see them appear again and again in other sections of this book, where they are used in particular situations.

What is your name?
Wie heissen Sie?
Vee his'-en zee?

My name is . . .
Ich heisse . . .
Içh is'-e . . .

What is his (her) name?
Wie heisst er (sie)?
Vee hist ehr (zee)?

I don't know.
Ich weiss nicht.
Iç vis niçt.

Do you know him (her)?
Kennen Sie ihn (sie)?
Ken'-en zee een (zee)?

Yes, I know him (her).
Ja, ich kenne ihn (sie).
Yah, iç ken'-e een (zee).

No, I don't know him (her).
Nein, ich kenne ihn (sie) nicht.
Nīn, iç ken'-e een (zee) niçt.

I know you.
Ich kenne Sie.
Iç ken'-e zee.

Where do you live?
Wo wohnen Sie?
Voh vohn'-en zee?

I live here.
Ich wohne hier.
Iç vohn'-e heer.

At which hotel are you staying?
In welchem Hotel wohnen Sie?
In vel'-çem hoh-tel' vohn'-en zee?

She's a beautiful woman.
Sie ist eine schöne Frau.
Zee ist īn'-e shöēn'-e frow.

She's a pretty girl.
Sie ist ein hübsches Mädchen.
Zee ist īn heüpsh'-es meht'-çen.

He's a handsome man.
Er is ein schöner Mann.
Ehr ist īn shöēn'-er mahn.

I love you.
Ich liebe dich.
Iç lee'-be diç.

I love her.
Ich liebe sie.
Iç lee'-be zee.

I love him.
Ich liebe ihn.
Iç lee'-be een.

Do you know where he lives?
Wissen Sie wo er wohnt?
Vis'-en zee voh ehr vohnt?

Do you speak English?
Sprechen Sie Englisch?
Shpreç'-en zee ehng'-leesh?

Please say it in English.
Bitte, sagen Sie es auf englisch.
Bit'-e, zah'-gen zee es owf ehng'-leesh.

Is there anyone here who speaks English?
Ist jemand hier, der Englisch spricht?
Ist yeh'-mahnt heer, dehr ehng'-leesh shpriçt?

Do you understand?
Verstehen Sie?
Fer-shteh'-en zee?

Yes, I understand.
Ja, ich verstehe.
Yah, iç fer-shteh'-e.

No, I don't understand.
Nein, ich verstehe nicht.
Nin, iç fer-shteh'-e niçt.

I understand a little.
Ich verstehe ein wenig.
Iç fer-shteh'-e in veh'-neeç.

I don't understand everything.
Ich verstehe nicht alles
Iç fer-shteh'-e niçt ahl'-es.

Please speak more slowly.
Bitte, sprechen Sie langsamer.
Bit'-e, shpreç'-en zee lahng'-zah-mer.

Please repeat.
Bitte, wiederholen Sie.
Bit'-e, vee'-der-hohl-en zee.

What did you say?
Was haben Sie gesagt?
Vahs hahb'-en zee ge-zahkht'?

How do you say that in German?
Wie sagt man das auf deutsch?
Vee zahkht mahn dahs owf doytch?

Bring me . . .
Bringen Sie mir . . .
Breeng'-en zee meer . . .

Tell me . . .
Sagen Sie mir . . .
Zahg'-en zee meer . . .

Give me . . .
Geben Sie mir . . .
Gehb'-en zee meer . . .

Show me . . .
Zeigen Sie mir . . .
Tsig'-en zee meer . . .

I need . . .
Ich brauche . . .
Iç browkh'-e . . .

I would like . . .
Ich möchte . . .
Iç möèç'-te . . .

I want . . .
Ich will . . .
Iç vil . . .

I don't want . . .
Ich will nicht . . .
Iç vil niçt . . .

I can do that.
Ich kann das machen.
Iç kahn dahs mahkh'-en.

I cannot do that.
Ich kann das nicht machen.
Iç kahn dahs niçt mahkh'-en.

Have you . . . ?
Haben Sie . . . ?
Hahb'-en zee . . . ?

Are you . . . ?
Sind Sie . . . ?
Zint zee . . . ?

Where is . . . ?
Wo ist . . . ?
Voh ist . . . ?

Where are . . . ?
Wo sind . . . ?
Voh zint . . . ?

Where are you going?
Wohin gehen Sie?
Voh-hin' geh'-en zee?

Where is he going?
Wohin geht er?
Voh-hin' geht ehr?

Where are we going?
Wohin gehen wir?
Voh-hin' geh'-en veer?

I will wait here.
Ich werde hier warten.
Iç ver'-de heer vahrt'-en.

What does that mean?
Was bedeutet das?
Vas be-doyt'-et dahs?

What do you mean?
Was meinen Sie?
Vahs min'-en zee?

You are right.
Sie haben Recht.
Zee hahb'-en reçt.

He is right.
Er hat Recht.
Ehr haht reçt.

You are wrong.
Sie haben Unrecht.
Zee hahb'-en un'-reçt.

He is wrong.
Er hat Unrecht.
Ehr haht un'-reçt.

Without doubt.
Ohne Zweifel.
Oh'-ne tsvi'-fel.

Send me . . .
Schicken (Senden) Sie mir . . .
Shik'-en (zend'-en) zee meer . . .

Write to me . . .
Schreiben Sie an mich . . .
Shrib'-en zee ahn miç . . .

How long must I wait?
Wie lange muss ich warten?
Vee lahng'-e mus iç vahrt'-en?

Wait here until I come back.
Warten Sie hier bis ich zurückkomme.
Vahrt'-en zee heer bis iç tsoo-rêuk'-kom-e.

Come here.
Kommen Sie her.
Kom'-en zee hehr.

Is it near here?
Ist es hier in der Nähe?
Ist es heer in dehr neh'-e?

Come in!
Herein!
Hehr-in'!

Is it far from here?
Ist es weit von hier?
Ist es vit fon heer?

It's possible.
Es ist möglich.
Es ist möêg'-leeç.

It's impossible.
Es ist unmöglich.
Es ist un-möêg'-leeç.

Emergencies

You will probably never need to use any of the brief cries, entreaties, or commands that appear here, but accidents do happen, items may be mislaid or stolen, and mistakes do occur. If an emergency does arise, it will probably be covered by one of these expressions.

Help!
Hilfe!
Heel'-fe!

Stop!
Halt!
Hahlt!

Help me!
Helfen Sie mir!
Hel'-fen zee meer!

Hurry up!
Beeilen Sie sich!
Be-i-len zee ziç!

There has been an accident!
Es ist ein Unfall geschehen!
Es ist in un'-fahl ge-sheh'-en!

Look out!
Passen Sie auf!
Pahs'-en zee owf!

Send for a doctor!
Lassen Sie einen Arzt kommen!
Lahs'-en zee in'-en ahrtst kom'-en!

Poison!
Gift!
Gift!

Fire!
Feuer!
Foy'-er!

Police!
Polizei!
Poh-lee-tsi'!

What happened?
Was ist geschehen?
Vahs ist ge-sheh'-en?

What's the matter?
Was ist los?
Vahs ist lohs?

Don't worry!
Machen Sie sich keine Sorgen!
Mahkh'-en zee ziç kin'-e zor'-gen!

I missed the train (bus, plane).
Ich habe den Zug (den Bus, das Flugzeug) verpasst.
Iç hahb'-e dehn tsook (dehn bus, dahs flook'-tsoykh) fer-pahst'.

I've been robbed!
Man hat mich bestohlen!
Mahn haht miç be-shtoh'-len!

That man stole my money!
Der Mann hat mir mein Geld gestohlen!
Dehr mahn haht meer min gelt ge-shtoh'-len!

Call the police!
Rufen Sie die Polizei!
Roof'-en zee dee poh-lee-tsi'!

I have lost my money!
Ich habe mein Geld verloren!
Iç hahb'-e min gelt fer-lor'-en!

I have lost my passport!
Ich habe meinen Reisepass verloren!
Iç hahb'-e min'-en ri'-ze-pahs fer-lohr'-en!

It's an American (British) passport.
Er ist ein amerikanischer (englischer) Reisepass.
Ehr ist in ah-meh-ree-kah'-neesh-er (ehng'-lee-sher) ri'-ze-pahs.

Stay where you are!
Bleiben Sie da wo Sie sind!
Blib'-en zee dah voh zee zint!

Don't move!
Bewegen Sie sich nicht!
Be-wehg'-en zee ziç niçt!

Signs
and
Notices

You could probably get along in a foreign land without speaking a word if only you could read the signs and notices that are posted and displayed as directions and advertising. A sign is an immediate communication to him who can read it, and the pronunciation doesn't matter. To help you in some usual situations, here are the common signs. Some of them will help you avoid embarrassment, and others danger. And some of them will merely make life more pleasant.

ABORT, Toilet
ACHTUNG, Warning
AUSFAHRT, Exit
AUSGANG, Exit
AUSKUNFT, Information
BAD, Bathroom
BADEZIMMER, Bathroom
BESETZT, Occupied

BLEIBEN SIE DRAUSSEN, Keep out
DAMEN, Women
DRÜCKEN, Push
EINBAHNSTRASSE, One way
EINFAHRT, Entrance
EINGANG, Entrance
EISENBAHNKREUZUNG, Railroad crossing
EINTRITT FREI, Admission free
ENGE BRÜCKE, Narrow bridge
ENGE STRASSE, Narrow road
ES IST GEFÄHRLICH, It's dangerous
FAHREN, Go
FEUER-MELDESTELLE, Fire alarm
FREI, Free
GEFAHR, Danger
GEFÄHRLICHTE KREUZUNG, Dangerous crossroad
GEFÄHRLICHE KURVE, Dangerous curve
GEÖFFNET, Open
GESCHLOSSEN, Closed
GESPERRT, No thoroughfare
HALT, Stop
HANDTÜCHER, Hand towels
HERREN, Men
KALT, Cold
KASSIERER, Cashier
KEIN PARKEN, No parking
KEIN TRINKWASSER, Do not drink the water
KEINE BIEGUNG NACH LINKS, No left turn
KEINE BIEGUNG NACH RECHTS, No right turn
KEINE DURCHFAHRT, No thoroughfare
KIRCHE, Church
KLINGELN, Ring

KURVE, Curve
LANGSAM, Slow
LANGSAM FAHREN, Go slow
MÖBLIERTE ZIMMER ZU VERMIETEN,
  Furnished rooms to let
NACH LINKS, To the left
NACH RECHTS, To the right
NICHT BERÜHREN, Do not touch
NICHT EINFAHREN, Do not enter
OFFEN, Open
PARKEN, Parking
RAUCHEN ERLAUBT, Smoking allowed
RAUCHEN VERBOTEN, No smoking
RECHTS FAHREN, Keep to the right
SCHULE, School
STEIGUNG, Hill
SPEISESAAL, Dining room
STOSSEN, Push
TOILETTE, Toilet
TRINKEN SIE DAS WASSER NICHT,
  Do not drink the water
UMLEITUNG, Detour
VERBOTEN, Forbidden
VORSICHT, Caution
WARM, Warm
WARNUNG, Warning
WARTEN, Wait
WARTESAAL, Waiting room
WASCHRAUM, Lavatory
ZIEHEN, Pull
ZOLL, Toll

Numbers, Time and Dates

You may only want to count your change or make an appointment or catch a train, but you will need to know the essentials of counting and telling time if you wish to stay on schedule, buy gifts, or pay for accommodations. In Europe, you should remember, time is told by a twenty-four hour system. Thus 10 P.M., in Germany, is 2200 and 10:30 P.M. is 2230.

Cardinal Numbers

one	**two**
eins	zwei
ins	*tsvi*
three	**four**
drei	vier
dri	*feer*
five	**six**
fünf	sechs
feŭnf	*zeks*

seven
sieben
zee'-ben

eight
acht
ahkht

nine
neun
noyn

ten
zehn
tsehn

eleven
elf
elf

twelve
zwölf
tsvöelf

thirteen
dreizehn
drī'-tsehn

fourteen
vierzehn
feer'-tsehn

fifteen
fünfzehn
fêunf'-tsehn

sixteen
sechzehn
seç'-tsehn

seventeen
siebzehn
zeep'-tsehn

eighteen
achtzehn
ahkht'-tsehn

nineteen
neunzehn
noyn'-tsehn

twenty
zwanzig
tsvahn'-tseeç

twenty-one
einundzwanzig
īn'-unt-tsvahn-tseeç

twenty-two
zweiundzwanzig
tsvī'-unt-tsvahn-tseeç

thirty
dreissig
drī'-seeç

thirty-one
einunddreissig
īn'-unt-drī-seeç

forty
vierzig
feer'-tseeç

fifty
fünfzig
fêunf'-tseeç

sixty
sechzig
zeç'-tseeç

seventy
siebzig
zeep'-tseeç

eighty
achtzig
ahkht'-tseeç

ninety
neunzig
noyn'-tseeç

one hundred
hundert
hun'-dert

two hundred
zweihundert
tsvī-hun'-dert

three hundred
dreihundert
drī-hun'-dert

five hundred
fünfhundert
feûnf-hun'-dert

one thousand
tausend
tow'-zent

one million
eine Million
ī'-ne meel-yohn'

ninteen hundred seventy- . . .
neunzehnhundert . . . undsiebzig
noyn-tsehn-hun'-dert . . . unt-zeep'-tseç

one man
ein Mann
īn mahn

one woman
eine Frau
īn'-e frow

one child
ein Kind
īn kint

two men
zwei Männer
tsvī men'-er

two woman
zwei Frauen
tsvī frow'-en

two children
zwei Kinder
tsvī kind-er

Some Ordinal Numbers

the first
der erste
dehr ehrs'-te

the second
der zweite
dehr tsvi'-te

the third
der dritte
dehr drit'-e

the fourth
der vierte
dehr feer'-te

the fifth
der fünfte
dehr feūnf'-te

the sixth
der sechste
dehr zeks'-te

the seventh
der siebente
dehr zee'-ben-te

the eighth
der achte
dehr ahkh'-te

the ninth
der neunte
dehr noyn'-te

the tenth
der zehnte
dehr tsehn'-te

the first man
der erste Mann
dehr ehrs'-te mahn

the first woman
die erste Frau
dee ehrs'-te frow

the first child
das erste Kind
dahs ehrs'-te kint

the fifth floor
der fünfte Stock
dehr feūnf'-te shtok

the third day
der dritte Tag
dehr drit'-e takh

the fourth street
die vierte Strasse
dee feer'-te shtrahs'-e

the second building
das zweite Gebäude
dahs tsvi'-te ge-boy'-de

Telling Time

What time is it?
Wieveil Uhr ist es?
Vee-feel' oor ist es?

It's one o'clock.
Es ist ein Uhr.
Es ist in oor.

It's two o'clock.
Es ist zwei Uhr.
Es ist tsvī oor.

It's a quarter after two.
Es ist Viertel nach zwei.
Es ist feer'-tel nahkh tsvī.

It's half-past two.
Es ist halb drei.
Es ist hahlp drī.

It's a quarter till two.
Es ist Viertel vor zwei.
Es ist feer'-tel for tsvī.

It's ten after two.
Es ist zehn nach zwei.
Es ist tsehn nahkh tsvī.

It's ten till two.
Es ist zehn vor zwei.
Es ist tsehn for tsvī.

It's five o'clock.
Es ist fünf Uhr.
Es ist feŭnf oor.

It's ten o'clock.
Es ist zehn Uhr.
Es ist tsehn oor.

It's noon.
Es ist Mittag.
Es ist mit'-tahkh.

It's midnight.
Es ist Mitternacht.
Es ist mit'-er-nahkht.

It's early.
Es ist früh.
Es ist freŭ.

It's late.
Es ist spät.
Es ist shpeht.

one second.
eine Sekunde.
īn'-e ze-kun'-de.

five seconds.
fünf Sekunden.
feŭnf ze-kun'-den.

one minute
eine Minute
in'-e mee-noo'-te

five minutes
fünf Minuten
feūnf mee-noo'-ten

one quarter hour
eine Viertelstunde
in'-e feer'-tel-shtun-de

one half hour
eine halbe Stunde
in'-e hahl'-be shtun'-de

one hour
eine Stunde
in'-e shtun'-de

five hours
fünf Stunden
feūnf shtun'-den

At what time are you leaving?
Um wieveil Uhr fahren Sie ab?
Um vee-feel' oor fahr'-en zee ahp?

When do you arrive?
Wann kommen Sie an?
Vahn kom'-en zee ahn?

When will we arrive?
Wann werden wir ankommen?
Vahn verd'-en veer ahn'-kom-em?

When shall we meet?
Wann werden wir uns treffen?
Vahn verd'-en veer oons tref'-en?

Meet me here at five o'clock.
Treffen Sie mich hier um fünf Uhr.
Tref'-en zee miç heer oom feūnf oor.

At what time do you get up?
Um wieviel Uhr stehen Sie auf?
Oom vee-feel' oor shteh'-en zee owf?

At what time do you go to bed?
Um wieviel Uhr gehen Sie ins Bett?
Oom vee-feel' oor geh'-en zee ins bet?

Dates

today
heute
hoy'-te

tomorrow
morgen
mor'-gen

yesterday
gestern
ges'-tern

one day
ein Tag
in tahkh

two days
zwei Tage
tsvi tah'-ge

five days
fünf Tage
feunf tah'-ge

the day after tomorrow
übermorgen
eu'-ber-mor-gen

the day before yesterday
vorgestern
for'-ges-tern

the morning
der Morgen
dehr mor'-gen

the afternoon
der Nachmittag
dehr nahkh'-mit-takh

the evening
der Abend
dehr ah'-bent

the night
die Nacht
dee nahkht

the week
die Woche
dee vo'-khe

the month
der Monat
dehr moh'-naht

the year
das Jahr
dahs yahr

last week
vorige Woche
for'-ee-ge vo'-khe

last month
vorigen Monat
for'-ee-gen moh'-naht

last year
voriges Jahr, letztes Jahr
for'-ee-ges yahr, lets'-tes yahr

this week
diese Woche
dee'-ze vo'-khe

this month
diesen Monat
dee'-zen moh'-naht

this year
dieses Jahr
dee'-zes yahr

next week
nächste Woche
nekhs'-te vo'-khe

next month
nächsten Monat
nekhs'-ten moh'naht

next year
nächstes Jahr
nekhs'-tes yahr

this morning
heute morgen
hoy'-te mor'-gen

yesterday morning
gestern morgen
ges'-tern mor'-gen

tomorrow morning
morgen früh
mor'-gen freü

this evening
heute abend
hoy'-te ah'-bent

yesterday evening
gestern abend
ges'-tern ah'-bent

tomorrow evening
morgen abend
mor'-gen ah'-bent

every day
jeden Tag
yeh'-den tahkh

two days ago
vor zwei Tagen
for tsvi tah'-gen

The Days of the Week

Monday
Montag
mohn'-tahkh

Tuesday
Dienstag
deens'-tahkh

Wednesday
Mittwoch
mit'-vokh

Thursday
Donnerstag
don'-ers-tahkh

Friday
Freitag
fri-tahkh

Saturday
Samstag
zahms'-tahkh

Sunday
Sonntag
zon'-tahkh

The Months of the Year

January
Januar
yah'-noo-ahr

February
Februar
feb'-roo-ahr

March
März
merts

April
April
ah-preel'

May
Mai
mi

June
Juni
yoo'-nee

July
Juli
yoo'-lee

August
August
ow-goost'

September
September
zep-tem'-ber

October
Oktober
ok-toh'-ber

November
November
noh-vem'-ber

December
Dezember
deh-tsem'-ber

The Seasons

the spring
der Frühling
dehr frü'-leeng

the summer
der Sommer
dehr zom'-er

the autumn
der Herbst
dehr herpst

the winter
der Winter
dehr vin'-ter

Changing Money

Whether poet or businessman, you will need cash as you travel. Sooner or later, every traveler meets the problem of how to manage the exchange. The following phrases cover most situations you will encounter. You will help yourself if you obtain the latest official exchange rate before you leave home, and it can do no harm if you familiarize yourself with the sizes, shapes, and even colors of the various coins and bills. It is wise, too, to take along a small amount of the foreign currency for immediate use on your arrival.

Where is the nearest bank?
Wo ist die nächste Bank?
Voh ist dee neçs'-te bahnk?

Please write the address.
Bitte, schreiben Sie die Anschrift (Adresse).
Bit'-e, shrib'-en zee dee ahn'-shrift (ah-dres'-e).

I would like to cash this check.
Ich möchte diesen Scheck einlösen.
Iç möç'-te deez'-en shek in'-löez-en.

Will you cash this check?
Wollen Sie diesen Scheck wechseln?
Vol'-en zee deez'-en shek veks'-eln?

Do you accept travelers' checks?
Nehmen Sie Reiseschecks an?
Nehm'-en zee ri'-ze-sheks ahn?

I want to change some money.	**What kind?**
Ich will was Geld wechseln.	Welche Art?
Iç vil wahs gelt veks'-eln.	*Vel'-çe ahrt?*
Dollars.	**Pounds.**
Dollar.	Pfunde.
Dol'-ahr.	*Pfun'-de.*

What is the rate of exchange for the dollar (pound)?
Was ist der Kurs für den Dollar (das Pfund)?
Vahs ist dehr kurs feür dehn dol'-ahr (dahs pfunt)?

Your passport, please.
Ihren Reisepass, bitte.
Ee'-ren riz'-e-pahs, bit'-e.

How much do you wish to change?
Wieviel wollen Sie wechseln?
Vee-feel' vol'-en zee veks'-eln?

I want to change ten dollars.
Ich will zehn Dollar wechseln.
Iç vil tsehn dol'-ahr veks'-eln.

Go to that clerk's window.
Gehen Sie zum Schalter jenes Angestellten.
Geh'-en zee tsum shahlt'-er yehn'-es ahn'-ge-shtelt-en.

Here's the money.
Hier ist das Geld.
Heer ist dahs gelt.

Please give me some small change.
Bitte, geben Sie mir etwas Kleingeld.
Bit'-e, gehb'-en zee meer et'-vahs klin'-gelt

Here's your change.
Hier ist Ihr Kleingeld.
Heer ist eer klin'-gelt.

Please count to see if it's right.
Bitte, zählen Sie es, um zu sehen ob es richtig ist.
Bit'-e, tsehl'-en zee es, um tsoo zeh'-en op es riç'-teeç ist.

Please sign this receipt.
Bitte, unterschreiben Sie diese Quittung.
Bit'-e, un'-ter-shrib-en zee deez'-e kvit'-ung.

Can I change money here at the hotel?
Kann ich hier im Hotel Geld wechseln?
Kahn iç heer im hoh-tel' gelt veks'-eln?

I'm expecting some money by mail.
Ich erwarte Geld mit der Post.
Iç ehr-wahr'-te gelt mit dehr post.

Customs

Your first experience with German may be with the personnel or fellow passengers on a ship or a plane, but you will really begin to use the language when you come to customs, Here are some phrases that will speed your entry into the country and get you on your way again.

Have you anything to declare?
Haben Sie etwas zu verzollen?
Hahb'-en zee et'-vahs tsoo fer-tsol'-en?

I have nothing to declare.
Ich habe nichts zu verzollen.
Iç hab'-e niçts tsoo fer-tsol'-en.

Your passport, please.
Ihren Reisepass, bitte.
Eer'-en ri'-ze-pahs, bit'-e.

Here is my passport.
Hier ist mein Reisepass.
Heer ist min ri'-ze-pahs.

Are these your bags?
Sind das Ihre Koffer?
Zint dahs eer'-e kof'-er?

Yes, and here are the keys:
Ja, und hier sind die Schlüssel.
Yah, unt heer zint dee shleûs'-el.

Open this box.
Machen Sie diese Schachtel auf.
Mahkh'-en zee deez'-e shahkh'-tel owf.

Have you any cigarettes or tobacco?
Haben Sie Zigaretten oder Tabak?
Hahb'-en zee tsee-gah-ret'-en oh'-der tah-bahk'?

I have only some cigarettes.
Ich habe nur einige Zigaretten.
Iç hab'-e noor i'-nee-ge tsee-gah-ret'-en.

Close your bags.
Machen Sie Ihre Koffer zu.
Mahkh'-en zee eer'-e kŏ)'-er tsoo.

You must pay duty.
Sie müssen Zoll bezahlen.
Zee meûs'-en tsol be-tsahl'-en.

They are for my personal use.
Die sind für meinen persönlichen Gebrauch.
Dee zint feûr min'-en per-zŏen'-leeç-en ge-browkh'.

How much must I pay?
Wieviel muss ich bezahlen?
Vee-feel' mus iç be-tsahl'-en?

You must pay . . .
Sie müssen . . . bezahlen.
Zee mêûs'-en . . . be-tsahl'-en.

May I go now?
Darf ich jetzt gehen?
Dahrf iç yetst geh'-en?

Is that all?
Ist das alles?
Ist dahs ahl'-es?

Porter, please carry this luggage.
Gepäckträger, bitte, tragen Sie dieses Gepäk.
Ge-pek'-treh-ger, bit'-e, trahg'-en zee deez'-es ge-pek'.

At the Hotel

Your accommodations may be a deluxe hotel, a modest hotel, a pension, or whatever, but it is important to be able to express your needs to be sure you get what you want. Outside of the cities, of course, few people are likely to be able to help you if you do not speak German, so we have given you the most useful expressions to cover most situations. They may make the difference between getting the room you want and having to settle for something less.

Which is the best hotel?
Welches ist das beste Hotel?
Vel'-çhes ist dahs best'-e hoh-tel'?

This is a good hotel.
Das ist ein gutes Hotel.
Dahs ist in goot'-es hoh-tel'.

I like this hotel.
Dieses Hotel gefällt mir.
Deez'-es hoh-tel' ge-felt' meer.

I would like to have a room here.
Ich möchte hier ein Zimmer nehmen.
Iç möeç'-te heer in tsim'-er nehm'-en.

A single room.
Ein Einzelzimmer.
īn īn'-tsel-tsim-er.

A double room.
Ein Zimmer mit zwei Betten.
īn tsim'-er mit tsvī bet'-en.

A room with (without) bath.
Ein Zimmer mit (ohne) Bad.
īn tsim'-er mit (oh-ne) baht.

Is there a shower?
Gibt es ein Brausebad?
Geept es īn brow'-ze-baht?

May I see the room?
Darf ich das Zimmer sehen?
Dahrf iç dahs tsim'-er zeh'-en?

This is a large room.
Das ist ein grosses Zimmer.
Dahs ist īn grohs'-es tsim'-er.

This room is too small.
Dieses Zimmer ist zu klein.
Deez'-es tsim'-er ist tsoo klīn.

The room faces the street.
Das Zimmer geht hinaus auf die Strasse.
Dahs tsim'-er geht hin-ows' owf dee shtrahs'-e.

Do you have a quieter room?
Haben Sie ein stilleres Zimmer?
Hahb'-en zee īn shtil'-er-es tsim'-er?

Do you have a room with a view of the ocean / court?
Haben Sie ein Zimmer mit Aussicht auf den Ozean / Hof?
Hahb'-en zee īn tsim'-er mit ows'-ziçt owf dehn oh-tseh-ahn' / hohf?

What is the price of this room?
Was ist der Preis fur dieses Zimmer?
Vahs ist dehr prīs fêur deez'-es tsim'-er?

That's much too expensive.
Das ist viel zu teuer.
Dahs ist feel tsoo toy'-er.

That's very good.
Das ist sehr gut.
Dahs ist zehr goot.

Does the price include breakfast?
Is das Frühstück im Preis einberechnet?
Is dahs freü'-shteük im pris in'-be-reçh-net?

Do you have a restaurant in the hotel?
Gibt es ein Restaurant im Hotel?
Geept es in res-toh-rahng' im hoh-tel'?

Must we eat our meals in the hotel restaurant?
Müssen wir unsere Mahlzeiten im Restaurant des Hotels
    essen?
*Meüs'-en veer un'-ze-re mahl'-tsit-en im res-toh-rahng' des
    hoh-tels' es'-en?*

Where is the dining room?
Wo ist der Speisesaal (das Esszimmer)?
Voh ist dehr shpi'-ze-zahl (dahs es'-tsim-er)?

We will stay here.
Wir werden hier bleiben.
Veer verd'-en heer blib'-en.

How long will you stay?
Wie lange werden Sie bleiben?
Vee lahng'-e verd'-en zee blib'-en?

I will stay three weeks.
Ich werde drei Wochen bleiben.
Iç verd'-e dri vokh'-en blib'-en.

We will stay three weeks.
Wir werden drei Wochen bleiben.
Veer verd'-en dri vokh'-en blib'-en.

Please fill out this card.
Bitte, füllen Sie diese Karte aus.
Bit'-e, feûl'-en zee deez'-e kahrt'-e ows.

My key, please.
Meinen Schlüssel, bitte.
Min'-en shleûs'-el, bit'-e.

What number, sir?
Welche Nummer, mein Herr?
Vel'-çe num'-er, min her?

I have lost my key.
Ich habe meinen Schlüssel verloren.
Iç hahb'-e min'-en shleûs'-el fer-lohr'-en.

Where is the key to my room?
Wo ist der Schlüssel für mein Zimmer?
Voh ist dehr shleûs'-el feûr min tsim'-er?

Where is the elevator?
Wo ist der Aufzug (Fahrstuhl)?
Voh ist dehr owf'-tsookh (fahr'-shtool)?

Take my suitcase to my room.
Tragen Sie meinen Koffer auf mein Zimmer.
Trahg'-en zee min'-en kof'-er owf min tsim'-er.

Where is the bathroom?
Wo ist das Badezimmer?
Voh ist dahs bah'-de-tsim-er?

Open the window, please.
Machen Sie das Fenster auf, bitte.
Mahkh'-en zee dahs fens'-ter owf, bit'-e.

Close the window, please.
Machen Sie das Fenster zu, bitte.
Mahkh'-en zee dahs fens'-ter tsoo, bit'-e.

Please call the chambermaid.
Lassen Sie das Zimmermädchen kommen, bitte.
Lahs'-en zee dahs tsim'-er-meht-çen kom'-en, bit'-e.

I want to have these shirts washed.
Ich möchte gern diese Hemden waschen lassen.
Iç möç'-te gern deez'-e hemd'-en vahsh'-en lahs'-en.

This is not my handkerchief.
Das ist nicht mein Taschentuch.
Dahs ist niçt min tahsh'-en-tookh.

I want a towel and some soap.
Ich möchte ein Handtuch und etwas Seife haben.
Iç möç'-te in hahnt'-tookh unt et'-vahs zi'-fe hahb'-en.

I want a clean towel.
Ich will ein sauberes Handtuch haben.
Iç vil in zowb'-er-es hahnt-tookh hahb'-en.

Please wake me at seven o'clock.
Bitte, wecken Sie mich um sieben Uhr.
Bit'-e, vek'-en zee miç um zeeb'-en oor.

We are leaving tomorrow.
Wir reisen morgen ab.
Veer riz'-en mor'-gen ahp.

Take my luggage down.
Tragen Sie mein Gepäck hinunter.
Trahg'-en zee min ge-pek' hin-unt'-er.

Are there any letters for me?
Sind Briefe für mich da?
Zint breef'-e feür miç dah?

I need some postage stamps.
Ich brauche einige Briefmarken.
Iç browkh'-e i'-nee-ge breef'-mahrk-en.

Using the Telephone

Most visitors to foreign lands are wary of using the telephone when they should not be. Of course, gesturing and pointing are of no avail when you cannot see the person to whom you are speaking and have to depend entirely on what you hear and say. Still, it is possible to communicate if you make an effort. If there is difficulty, remember to ask the other person to speak slowly. It's your best assurance that the message will get through.

Where is there a telephone?
Wo ist ein Fernsprecher?
Voh ist in fern'-shprech-er?

I would like to telephone.
Ich möchte anrufen (telefonieren).
Iç möeç'-te ahn'-roof-en (tel-leh-foh-neer'-en).

I would like to make a call to . . .
Ich möchte ein Ferngespräch nach . . . machen.
Iç möeç'-te in fern'-ge-shpreç nahkh . . . mahkh'-en.

What is the telephone number?
Was ist die Telefonnummer?
Vahs ist dee teh-leh-fohn'-num-er?

Where is the telephone book?
Wo ist das Telefonadressbuch?
Voh ist dahs teh-leh-fohn-ah-dres'-bookh?

My number is . . .
Meine Nummer ist . . .
Min'-e num'-er ist . . .

Operator!
Fräulein!
Froy'-lin!

I want number . . .
Ich brauche Nummer . . .
Iç browkh'-e num'-er . . .

Can I dial this number?
Kann ich diese Nummer wählen?
Kahn iç deez'-e num'-er vehl'-en?

How much is a telephone call to . . . ?
Was kostet ein Telefongespräch nach . . . ?
Vahs kost'-et in teh-leh-fohn'-ge-shpreç nahkh . . . ?

I am ringing.
Ich rufe an.
Iç roof'-e ahn.

Please do not hang up.
Bitte, bleiben Sie am Apparat.
Bit'-e, blib'-en zee ahm ah-pah-raht'.

Deposit coins.
Bitte, Münzen einzahlen.
Bit'-e, meün'-tsen in'-tsahl-en.

They do not answer.
Sie antworten nicht.
Zee ahnt'-vort-en niçt.

Please dial again.
Bitte, wählen Sie wieder.
Bit'-e, vehl'-en zee vee'-der.

The line is busy.
Die Linie ist besetzt.
Dee leen'-yeh ist be-zetst'.

Who is speaking?
Wer spricht?
Vehr shpriçt?

May I speak to . . . ?
Darf ich . . . sprechen?
Dahrf iç . . shpreç'-en?

He (she) is not in.
Er (sie) ist nicht hier.
Ehr (zee) ist niçt heer.

Please speak more slowly.
Bitte, sprechen Sie langsamer.
Bit'-e, shreç'-en zee lahng'-zah-mer.

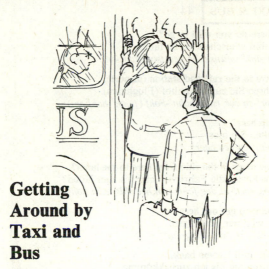

Getting Around by Taxi and Bus

The drivers of taxis and buses almost never speak English, which may be fortunate when you relish a few peaceful moments. However, you will have to tell them where you're going, or want to go, and for that we've provided some handy phrases.

Call a taxi, please.
Holen Sie eine Taxe, bitte.
Hohl'-en zee in'-e tahks'-e, bit'-e.

Put my luggage into the taxi.
Bringen Sie mein Gepäck in die Taxe.
Breeng'-en zee min ge-pek' in dee tahks'-e.

Driver, are you free?
Fahrer, sind Sie frei?
Fahr'-er, zint zee fri?

Where do you wish to go?
Wohin wünschen Sie zu fahren?
Voh-hin' věunsh'-en zee tsoo fahr'-en?

Drive to the railroad station (airport).
Fahren Sie zum Bahnhof (Flughafen).
Fahr'-en zee tsum bahn'-hohf (flook'-hahf-en.)

Stop here!
Halten Sie hier!
Hahlt'-en zee heer!

How much is the ride from here to the hotel?
Was kostet die Fahrt von hier bis zum Hotel?
Vahs kost'-et dee fahrt von heer bis tsum hoh-tel'?

I want to get out here.
Ich will hier aussteigen.
Iç vil heer ows'-shtīg-en.

Wait until I come back.
Warten Sie bis ich zurückkomme.
Vahrt'-en zee bis iç tsoo-rěuk'-kom-e.

Wait for me here.
Warten Sie hier auf mich.
Vahrt'-en zee heer owf miç.

Drive a little farther.
Fahren Sie ein bisschen weiter.
Fahr'-en zee in bis'-çen vīt'-er.

Please drive carefully.
Bitte, fahren Sie mit Vorsicht.
Bit'-e, fahr'-en zee mit for'-ziçt.

Please drive slowly.
Bitte, fahren Sie langsam.
Bit'-e, fahr'-en zee lahng-zahm.

Turn to the left (right) here.
Hier links (rechts) einbiegen.
Heer leenks (reçts) in'-beeg-en.

Drive straight ahead.
Fahren Sie geradeaus.
Fahr'-en zee ge-rah-de-ows'.

How much is the fare?
Was kostet die Fahrt?
Vahs kost'-et dee fahrt?

Which bus goes downtown?
Welcher Bus fährt zur Stadtmitte?
Velç'-er bus fehrt tsur shtaht'-mit-e?

Bus number . . .
Der Bus Nummer . . .
Dehr bus num'-er . . .

Does the bus stop here?
Hält der Bus hier?
Helt dehr bus heer?

Please tell me when we arrive at . . . street.
Bitte, sagen Sie mir wenn wir in die . . . Strasse ankommen.
Bit'-e, sahg'-en zee meer ven veer in dee . . . shtrahs'-e ahn'-kom-en.

Which bus goes to . . . ?
Welcher Bus fährt nach . . . ?
Velç'-er bus fehrt nahkh . . . ?

Get on the bus here.
Steigen Sie hier in den Bus ein.
Shtig'-en zee heer in dehn bus in.

Get off the bus here.
Steigen Sie hier vom Bus aus.
Shtig'-en zee heer fom bus ows.

Does this bus go to the museum?
Fährt dieser Bus zum Museum?
Fährt deez'-er bus tsum moo-zeh'-oom?

Where must I transfer?
Wo muss ich umsteigen?
Voh mus iç um'-shtig-en?

When does the last bus leave?
Wann fährt der letzte Bus ab?
Vahn fehrt dehr letst'-e bus ahp?

Eating and Drinking

Merely going abroad is thrill enough for some persons; for others the high points are likely to be the hours spent at the table. Getting to know and appreciate the national cuisine and learning how to order the native dishes are extra thrills for many travelers. Here, to the phrases that are necessary to order your meals, we have added a menu reader of the most typical dishes of the cuisine in the countries where German is spoken.

I'm hungry.
Ic habe Hunger.
Iç hahb'-e hung'-er.

I'm thirsty.
Ich habe Durst.
Iç hahb'-e durst.

Are you hungry?
Haben Sie Hunger?
Hahb'-en zee hung'-er?

Are you thirsty?
Haben Sie Durst?
Hahb'-en zee durst?

I'm not hungry.
Ich habe keinen Hunger.
Iç hahb'-e kin'-en hung'-er.

I'm not thirsty.
Ich habe keinen Durst.
Iç hahb'-e kin'-en durst.

Do you want to eat now?
Wollen Sie jetzt essen?
Vol'-en zee yetst es'-en?

Let's eat now.
Essen wir jetzt.
Es'-en veer yetst.

Where is there a good restaurant?
Wo ist ein gutes Restaurant (Speisehaus)?
Voh is in goot'-es res-toh-rahng' (shpi'-ze-hows)?

The meals.
Die Mahlzeiten.
Dee mahl'-tsit-en.

breakfast
das Frühstück
dahs freû'-shteûk

lunch
das Mittagessen
dahs mit'-tahk-es-en

dinner
das Abendessen
dahs ah'-bent-es-en

supper
das Abendessen
dahs ah'-bent-es-en

At what time is breakfast (lunch, dinner)?
Um wieviel Uhr speist man Frühstück (Mittagessen, Abendessen)?
Um vee-feel' oor shpist mahn freû'-shteûk (mit'-tahk-es-en ah'-bent-es-en)?

I want breakfast (lunch, dinner) in my room.
Ich möchte in meinem Zimmer frühstücken (Mittagessen, Abendessen).
Iç möeç'-te in min'-em tsim'-er freû'-shteûk-en (mit'-tahk-es-en, ah'-bent-es-en).

Breakfast is ready.
Das Frühstück ist fertig.
Dahs freû'-shteûk ist fer'-teeç.

I would like . . .
Ich möchte . . .
Iç möeç'-te . . .

eggs
Eier
i'-er

fried eggs
Spiegeleier
shpee'-gel-i-er

scrambled eggs
Rühreier
réûr'-i-er

two soft-boiled eggs
zwei weichgekochte Eier
tsvi viç'-ge-kokh-te i'-er

a poached egg
ein Ei ohne Schale
in i oh'-ne shah'-le

bacon
Speck
shpek

bread and butter
Brot and Butter
broht unt but'-er

black coffee
schwarzen Kaffee
shvarts'-en Kah-feh'

coffee with milk
Kaffee mit Milch
kah-feh' mit milç

coffee without milk
Kaffee ohne Milch
kah-feh' oh'-ne milç

milk
Milch
milç

tea
Tee
teh

ham
Schinken
sheen'-ken

cold meat
kaltes Fleisch
kahlt'-es flish

rolls
Brötchen
brôèt'-çen

Dinner is being served.
Das Abendessen ist angerichtet.
Dahs ah'-bent-es-en ist ahn'-ge-riçt-et.

A table for two, please.
Einen Tisch für zwei, bitte.
Īn'-en tish feúr tsvī, bit'-e.

Where is the waitress?
Wo ist die Kellnerin?
Voh ist dee kel'-ner-in?

Waiter (Waitress), the menu, please.
Kellner (Kellnerin), die Speisekarte, bitte.
Kel'-ner (kel'-ner-in), dee shpī'-ze-kahr-te, bit'-e.

Waiter, please bring an ashtray.
Kellner, bitte, bringen Sie einen Aschenbecher.
Kel'-ner, bit'-e, breeng'-en zee īn'-en ah'-shen-beç-er.

What do you recommend?
Was empfehlen Sie?
Vahs emp-fehl'-en zee?

Do you recommend . . . ?
Empfehlen Sie . . . ?
Emp-fehl'-en zee . . . ?

Bring me some coffee now, please.
Bitte, bringen Sie mir Kaffee jetzt.
Bit'-e, breeng'-en zee meer kah-feh' yetst.

More butter, please.
Mehr Butter, bitte.
Mehr but'-er, bit'-e.

Bring some more sugar.
Bringen Sie noch mehr Zucker.
Breeng'-en zee nokh mehr tsuk'-er.

Bring me a glass of water, please.
Bitte, bringen Sie mir ein Glas Wasser.
Bit'-e, breeng'-en zee meer in glahs vahs'-er.

This coffee is cold.
Dieser Kaffee ist kalt.
Deez'-er kah-feh' ist kahlt.

Do you take milk and sugar?
Nehmen Sie Milch und Zucker?
Nehm'-en zee milç unt tsuk'-er?

No sugar, thank you.
Keinen Zucker, danke.
Kin'-en tsuk'-er, dahnk'-e.

We eat only fruit at breakfast.
Wir essen nur Obst zum Frühstück.
Veer es'-en noor ohpst tsum frêu'-shtêuk.

This butter is not fresh.
Diese Butter ist nicht frisch.
Deez'-e but'-er ist niçt frish.

This milk is warm.
Diese Milch ist warm.
Deez'-e milç ist vahrm.

This milk is sour.
Diese Milch ist sauer.
Deez'-e milç ist zow'-er.

I would like a glass of cold milk.
Ich möchte ein Glas kalte Milch haben.
Iç môeç'-te in glahs kahlt'-e milç hahb'-en.

The Condiments

the salt
das Salz
dahs zahlts

the pepper
der Pfeffer
dehr pfef'-er

the sugar
der Zucker
dehr tsuk'-er

the oil
das Öl
dahs ôel

the vinegar
der Essig
dehr es'-eeç

the mustard
der Senf, der Mostrich
dehr zenf, dehr mosh'-treeç

Another cup of coffee?
Noch eine Tasse Kaffee?
Nokh in'-e tahs'-e kah-feh'?

Another cup of tea?
Noch eine Tasse Tee?
Nokh in'-e tahs'-e teh?

Do you want some more tea?
Wollen Sie mehr Tee?
Vol'-en zee mehr teh?

Nothing more, thank you.
Nichts mehr, danke.
Niçts mehr, dahnk'-e.

At what time are the meals in this hotel?
Um wieviel Uhr werden die Mahlzeiten in diesem Hotel serviert?
Um vee-feel' oor verd'-en dee mahl'-tsit-en in deez'-em hoh-tel' ser-veert'?

We dine at seven o'clock.
Wir speisen um sieben Uhr.
Veer shpiz'-en um zeeb'-en oor.

Foods and Beverages

the fish
der Fisch
dehr fish

the meat
das Fleisch
dahs flish

fruit
das Obst (die Frucht, die Früchte)
dahs ohpst (dee frookht, dee freuçt'-e)

vegetables
das Gemüse
dahs ge-meuz'-e

the water.
das Wasser
dahs vahs'-er

the wine
der Wein
dehr vin

the beer
das Bier
dahs beer

Here they dine at eight o'clock.
Hier speist man um acht Uhr.
Heer shpist mahn um ahkht oor.

Please reserve a table for us.
Bitte, belegen Sie einen Tisch für uns.
Bit'-e, be-lehg'-en zee in'-en tish feûr uns.

Do you want soup?
Wünschen Sie Suppe?
Véûnsh'-en zee zup'-e?

Bring me a fork (a knife) (a spoon).
Bringen Sie mir eine Gabel (ein Messer) (einen Löffel).
Breeng'-en zee meer in'-e gahb'-el (in mes'-er) (in'-en löef'-el).

This fork is dirty.
Diese Gabel ist schmutzig.
Deez'-e gahb'-el ist shmuts'-eeç.

---

the cheese
der Käse
dehr keh'-ze

the bread
das Brot
dahs broht

the butter
die Butter
de but'-er

the milk
die Milch
dee milç

the jam
die Marmelade
dee mahr-me-lah'-de

the honey
der Honig
dehr hoh'-neeç

the soup
die Suppe
dee zup'-e

the salad
der Salat
dehr zah-laht'

This spoon isn't clean.
Dieser Löffel ist nicht sauber.
Deez'-er lö͞ef'-el ist niçt zow'-ber.

Please bring me a napkin.
Bitte, bringen Sie mir eine Serviette.
Bit'-e, breeng'-en zee meer in'-e ser-vee-et'-e.

I would like a glass of wine.
Ich möchte ein Glas Wein haben.
Iç mö͞eç'-te in glahs vin hahb'-en.

A glass of red (white) wine.
Ein Glas Rot- (Weiss-)wein.
In glahs roht- (vis-) vin.

A bottle of wine.
Eine Flasche Wein.
In'-e flahsh'-e vin.

The Setting

a spoon
ein Löffel
in lö͞ef'-el

a small spoon
ein kleiner Löffel
in klin'-er lö͞ef'-el

a knife
ein Messer
in mes'-er

a small knife
ein kleines Messer
in klin'-es mes'-er

a fork
eine Gabel
in'-e gahb'-el

a small fork
eine kleine Gabel
in'-e klin'-e gahb'-el

a plate
ein Teller
in tel'-er

a tray
ein Tablett, ein Servierbrett
in tah-blet', in ser-veer'-bret

a napkin
eine Serviette
in'-e ser-vee-et'-e

A half bottle.
Eine halbe Flasche.
Īn'-e hahlb'-e flahsh'-e.

This wine is too warm.
Dieser Wein ist zu warm.
Deez'-er vin ist tsoo vahrm.

Please bring some ice.
Bitte, bringen Sie etwas Eis.
Bit'-e, breeng'-en zee et'-vahs is.

I didn't order this.
Das habe ich nicht bestellt.
Dahs hahb'-e iç niçt be-shtelt'.

A glass of beer.
Ein Glas Bier.
Īn glahs beer.

A bottle of beer.
Eine Flasche Bier.
Īn'-e flahsh'-e beer.

To your health!
Prosit!
Proh'-zit!

Enjoy your meal!
Guten Appetit!
Goot'-en ah-pe-teet'!

This tablecloth is not clean.
Dieses Tischtuch ist nicht sauber.
Deez'-es tish'-tookh ist niçt zow'-ber.

Do you eat fish?
Essen Sie Fisch?
Es'-en zee fish?

He doesn't eat meat.
Er isst kein Fleisch.
Ehr ist kin flish.

I don't eat dessert.
Ich esse keinen Nachtisch.
Iç es'-e kin'-en nahkh'-tish.

He would like some ice cream.
Er möchte Rahmeis haben.
Ehr möeç'-te rahm'-is hahb'-en.

Waiter, the check, please.
Kellner, die Rechnung, bitte.
Kel'-ner, dee reç'-noong, bit'-e.

How much do I owe you?
Wieviel bin ich Ihnen schuldig?
Vee-feel' bin iç ee'-nen shool'-deeç?

Is the tip included?
Ist de Bedienung mitberechnet?
Ist dee be-dee'-noong mit'-be-reç-net?

Where do I pay?
Wo bezahle ich?
Voh be-tsahl'-e iç?

At the cashier's booth.
An der Kasse.
Ahn dehr kahs'-e.

I have already paid.
Ich habe schon bezahlt.
Iç hahb'-e shohn be-tsahlt'.

Here is a tip.
Hier ist Trinkgeld.
Heer ist treenk'-gelt.

I left the tip on the table.
Ich habe das Trinkgeld auf dem Tisch gelassen.
Iç hahb'-e dahs treenk'-gelt owf dehm tish ge-lahs'-en.

There is a mistake in the bill.
Es ist ein Irrtum in der Rechnung.
Es ist in eer'-toom in dehr reç'-noong.

Menu
Reader

Suppen Soups

Erbsensuppe (*erp'-sen-zup-e*) Pea soup.

Gemüsesuppe (*ge-meûz'-e-zup-e*) Vegetable soup.

Kartoffel suppe (*kahr-tof'-el-zup-e*) Potato soup.

Königinsuppe (*kôe'-nee-gin-zup-e*) Cream of chicken soup.

Kraftbrühe (*krahft'-breû-e*) Consomme.

Leberknödelsuppe (*leh'-ber-kôed-el-zup-e*) Liver dumpling soup.

Linsensuppe (*lin'-zen-zup-e*) Lentil soup.

Ochsenschwanzsuppe (*ok'-sen-shvahnts-zup-e*) Oxtail soup.

Fisch Fish

Forelle (*for-el'-e*) Trout.
Hecht (*heçt*) Pike.
Lachs (*lahks*) Salmon.
Makrele (*mah-kreh'-le*) Mackerel.
Rheinsalm (*rin'-zahlm*) Rhine salmon.
Schellfisch (*shel'-fish*) Haddock.
Seezunge (*zeh'-tsung-e*) Sole.

Fleisch Meat

Aufschnitt (*owf'-shnit*) Cold cuts.
Beefsteak (*beef'-shtehk*) Steak.
   Englisch (*ehng'-leesh*) Rare.
   gut durchgebraten (*goot doorç'-ge-braht-en*) Well done.
Brathuhn (*braht'-hoon*) Roast chicken.
Bratwurst (*braht'-voorst*) Grilled sausage.
Deutsches Beefsteak (*doytch'-es beef'-shtehk*) Hamburger
   steak.
Eisbein (*is'-bin*) Pig's knuckles.
Gefüllte Kalbsbrust (*ge-feul'-te kahlps'-brust*) Stuffed
   breast of veal.
Hammelkotelett (*Hahm'-el-kot-let*) Lamb chops.
Kalbsfleisch (*kahlps'-flish*) Veal.
Kaltes Geflügel (*kahlt'-es ge-fleug'-el*) Cold poultry.
Kassler Rippchen (*kahs'-ler rip'-çen*) Smoked pork chops.
Leber (*leh'-ber*) Liver.
Leberkäse (*leh'-ber-keh-ze*) Liver-cheese meatloaf.
Schmorgericht (*shmohr'-ge-riçt*) Stew.
Rindfleisch (*rint'-flish*) Beef.
Rinderbraten (*rind'-er-braht-en*) Roast beef.
Sauerbraten (*zow'-er-braht-en*) Sauerbraten.
Schinken (*sheenk'-en*) Ham.
Schweinebraten (*shvin'-e-braht-en*) Roast pork.
Wienerschnitzel (*veen'-er-shnits-el*) Veal cutlet.
Wurst (*vurst*) Sausage.
Weisswurst (*vis'-vurst*) White sausage.

Gemüse und Salaten Vegetables and Salads

Artischocken (*ahr-tee-shok'-en*) Artichokes.
Blumenkohl (*bloom'-en-kohl*) Cauliflower.
Bohnen (*bohn'-en*) Beans.
Erbsen (*erps'-en*) Peas.
Gemischter Salat (*ge-misht'-er zah-laht'*) Mixed Salad.
Gurkensalat (*goork'-en-zah-laht*) Cucumber salad.
Kartoffelsalat (*kahr-tof'-el-zah-laht*) Potato salad.
Knödel (*knöed'-el*) Dumplings.
Kopfsalat (*kopf'-zah-laht*) Lettuce salad.
Mohrrüben (*mohr'-rēūb-en*) Carrots.
Rohkostplatte (*roh'-kost-plaht-e*) Raw vegetable salad.
Nudeln (*nood'-eln*) Noodles.
Rote Rüben (*roht'-e rēūb'-en*) Beets.
Rotkohl (*roht'-kohl*) Red Cabbage.
Salzkartoffeln (*sahlts'-kahr-tof-eln*) Boiled potatoes.
Sauerkraut (*zow'-er-krowt*) Sauerkraut.
Sellerie (*zel-e-ree'*) Celery.
Spargel (*shpahr'-gel*) Asparagus.
Pilze (*peelts'-e*) Mushrooms.
Vorspeisen (*for'-shpīz-en*) Hors d'oeuvres.
Weisse Rüben (*vīs'-e rēūb'-en*) Turnips.

Nachtisch und Obst Dessert and Fruit

Ananas (*ah-nah-nahs'*) Pineapple.
Äpfel (*epf'-el*) Apples.
Apfelsinen (*ahpf'-el-zeen-en*) Oranges.
Bananen (*bah-nahn'-en*) Bananas.
Birnen (*beern'-en*) Pears.
Blätterteiggebäck (*blet'-er-tikh-ge-bek*) Puff pastry.
Bratapfel (*braht'-ahpf-el*) Baked apple.
Eis, Rahmeis (*īs, rahm'-īs*) Ice cream.
Käse (*keh'-ze*) Cheese.
Kirschen (*keersh'-en*) Cherries.
Kompott (*kop-pot'*) Stewed fruit.
Kuchen (*kookh'-en*) Cake.

Pfannkuchen (*pfahn'-kookh-en*) Sugared pancakes.
Pfirsiche (*pfeer'-zeeç-e*) Peaches.
Teegebäck (*teh'-ge-bek*) Tea cakes.
Torten (*tort'-en*) Pastries.
Weintrauben (*vin'-trowb-en*) Grapes.

Getränke Beverages

Apfelsaft (*ahpf'-el-zahft*) Cider.
Bier (*beer*) Beer.
   ein Dunkles (*in dunk'-les*) A dark beer.
   ein Helles (*in hel'-es*) A light beer.
Kaffee (*kah-feh'*) Coffee.
Milch (*milç*) Milk.
Rotwein (*roht'-vin*) Red wine.
Schnaps (*shnahps*) Brandy.
Schokolade (*shoh-koh-lah'-de*) Chocolate.
Sekt (*zekt*) Champagne.
Tee (*teh*) Tea.
Tomatensaft (*toh-maht'-en-zahft*) Tomato juice.
Wasser (*vahs'-er*) Water.
Weisswein (*vis'-vin*) White wine.

Shopping

Shopping abroad is always an adventure and frequently a delight. It's not only the varied merchandise that you may buy to take home as gifts, but the sheer pleasure of making yourself understood. It's important to know, and to be able to explain, exactly what it is that you want, since, obviously, you won't be able to trot downtown a week later to make an exchange. You'll discover, too, that sizes and weights are different; so we have included conversion tables here. Here are the typical questions that you or the salesman might ask or the statement you may make during your shopping trips.

I would like to go shopping.
Ich möchte einkaufen gehen.
Iç möç'-te in'-kowf-en geh'-en.

At what time do the stores open (close)?
Um wieviel Uhr werden die Kaufläden (Geschäfte) geöffnet (geschlossen)?
Um vee-feel' oor verd'-en dee kowf'-lehd-en (ge-sheft'-e) ge-öf'-net (ge-shlos'-en)?

Where is there . . . ?
Wo ist . . . ?
Voh ist . . . ?

an antique shop.
ein Antiquitätenladen.
*in ahn-tee-kvee-teht'-en-
  lahd-en.*

a book store.
eine Buchhandlung.
in'-e bookh'-hahnt-loong.

a candy store.
eine Zuckerbäckerei.
in'-e tsuk'-er-bek-er-i.

a department store.
ein Warenhaus.
in wahr'-en-hows.

a dressmaker.
eine Schneiderin.
in'-e shnid'-er-in.

a druggist.
ein Apotheker.
in ah-poh-tehk'-er.

a drugstore.
eine Apotheke.
in'-e ah-poh-tehk'-e.

a florist.
ein Blumenhändler.
in bloom'-en-hent-ler.

a grocery.
ein Lebensmittelgeschäft.
in lehb'-ens-mit-el-ge-sheft.

a greengrocer.
ein Gemüsehändler.
in ge-meûz'-e-hent-ler.

a hat shop.
ein Hutgeschäft.
in hoot'-ge-sheft.

a jewelry store.
eine Juwelenhändlung.
*in'-e yoo-wehl'-en-hahnt-
  loong.*

a perfumery.
ein Parfümladen.
in pahr-feûm'-lahd-en.

a photography shop.
ein Photographieladen.
*in foh-toh-grah-fee'-lahd-
  en.*

May I help you?
Womit kann ich dienen?
Voh-mit' kahn iç deen'-en?

Will you help me, please?
Wollen Sie mir helfen, bitte?
Vol'-en zee meer helf'-en, bit'-e?

Are you being served?
Werden Sie bedient?
Verd'-en zee be-deent'?

What do you wish?
Was wünschen Sie?
Vahs veūnsh'-en zee?

Do you sell . . . ?
Verkaufen Sie . . . ?
Fer-kowf'-en zee . . . ?

Do you have . . . ?
Haben Sie . . . ?
Hahb'-en zee . . . ?

Please show me some . . .
Bitte, zeigen Sie mir einige . . .
Bit'-e, tsig'-en zee meer i'-nee-ge . . .

What size, please?
Welche Grösse, bitte?
Vel'-çe grōēs'-e, bit'-e?

Try on these . . .
Probieren Sie diese . . .
Proh-beer'-en zee deez'-e . . .

---

a shoe store.
ein Schuhgeschäft.
in shoo'-ge-sheft.

a tailor.
ein Schneider.
in shnid'-er.

a tobacconist.
ein Tabakhändler / Zigarrenladen.
in tah-bahk'-hent-ler / tsee-gahr'-en-lahd-en.

a toy store.
ein Spielzeuggeschäft.
in shpeel'-tsoykh-ge-sheft.

a watchmaker.
ein Uhrmacher.
in oor'-mahkh-er.

I would like . . .
Ich möchte . . .
Iç mбeç'-te . . .

a brassiere
ein Büstenhalter
in bêus'-ten-hahlt-er

a handkerchief
ein Taschentuch
in tahsh'-en-tookh

panties
Unterhose
un'-ter-hoh-ze

shoes
Schuhe
shoo'-e

a skirt
ein Rock
in rok

socks
Socken
zok'-en

a suit
ein Anzug
in ahn'-tsookh

a tie
eine Krawatte
in'-e krah-vaht'-e

underwear
Unterzeug, Unterwäsche
un'-ter-tsoykh, un'-ter-vesh-e

gloves
Handschuhe
hahnt'-shoo-e

a hat
ein Hut
in hoot

a shirt
ein Hemd
in hemt

shorts
kurze Hose
kurts'-e hoh'-ze

a slip
ein Unterrock
in un'-ter-rok

stockings
Strümpfe
shtrêumpf'-e

a sweater
ein Pullover
in pul-oh'-ver

an undershirt
ein Unterhemd
in un'-ter-hemt

I would like to buy . . .
Ich möchte . . . kaufen.
Iç möèc'-te . . . kowf'-en.

a battery	**a camera**
eine Batterie	ein Photoapparat
in'-e bah-te-ree'	*in foh'-toh-ah-pah-raht*
film	**flashbulbs**
Film	Photobirnen
film	*foh'-toh-beern-en*
a pen	**a pencil**
eine Feder	ein Bleistift
in'-e fehd'-er	*in bli'-shtift*
postcards	**stamps**
Postkarten	Briefmarken
post'-kahrt-en	*breef'-mahrk-en*
lotion	**powder**
Hautwasser	Puder, Gesichtspuder
howt'-vahs-er	*pood'-er, ge-ziçts'-pood-er*
razor blades	**shampoo**
Rasierklingen	Haarwaschen
rah-zeer'-kleeng-en	*hahr'-vahsh-en*
shaving cream	**soap**
Rasiercreme	Seife
rah-zeer'-kreh-me	*zi'-fe*
toothbrush	**toothpaste**
Zahnbürste	Zahnpasta
tsahn'-béûrs-te	*tsahn'-pahs-tah*

How much does it cost?
Wieviel kostet es?
Vee-feel' kost'-et es?

How much do they cost?
Wieviel kosten sie?
Vee-feel' kost'-en zee?

That is too expensive.
Das ist zu teuer.
Dahs ist tsoo toy'-er.

That is cheap.
Das ist billig.
Dahs ist bil-eeç.

I like this one.
Dieser gefällt mir.
Deez'-er ge-felt' meer.

I will take this one.
Ich werde diesen nehmen.
Iç verd'-e deez'-en nehm'-en.

This dress is too short.
Dieses Kleid ist zu kurz.
Deez'-es klīt ist tsoo kurts.

This skirt is too long.
Dieser Rock ist zu lang.
Deez'-er rok ist tsoo lahng.

I would like to see a white shirt.
Ich möchte ein weisses Hemd sehen.
Iç möeç'-te in vis'-es hemt zeh'-en.

He would like to see some white shirts.
Er möchte einige weisse Hemden sehen.
Ehr möeç'-te i'-nee-ge vis'-e hemd'-en zeh'-en.

cigars Zigarren *tsee-gahr'-en*	**cigarettes** Zigaretten *tsee-gah-ret'-en*
flint Feuerstein *foy'-er-shtin*	**fluid** Flüssigkeit *fleûs'-eeç-kit*
lighter ein Feuerzeug *in foy'-er-tsoykh*	**matches** Streichhölzer, Zündhölzer *shtriç'-höelts-er, tseûnt'-höelts-er*

I don't like this color.
Diese Farbe gefällt mir nicht.
Deez'-e fahrb'-e ge-felt' meer niçt.

Have you a lighter (darker) blue dress?
Haben Sie ein helleres (dunkeleres) blaues Kleid?
Hahb'-en zee in hel'-er-es (doonk'-ler-es) blow'es klit?

I prefer it in. . . .
Ich ziehe es in. . . vor.
Iç tsee'-e es in. . . . for.

---

black	**blue**	**brown**
schwarz	blau	braun
shvahrts	*blow*	*brown*
gray	**green**	**red**
grau	grün	rot
grow	*greun*	*roht*
white	**yellow**	
weiss	gelb	
vis	*gelp*	
dark	**light**	
dunkel	hell	
dunk'-el	*hel*	

Sale
Verkauf
Fer-kowf'

For Sale
Zu verkaufen
Tsoo fer-kowf'-en

Clearance Sale
Räumungsausverkauf
Roy-moongs-ows'-fer-kowf

The sleeves are too wide.
Die Ärmel sind zu breit.
Dee erm'-el zint tsoo brit.

The sleeves are too narrow.
Die Ärmel sind zu eng (schmal).
Dee erm'-el zint tsoo ehng (shmahl).

I would like to see some shoes.
Ich möchte Schuhe sehen.
Iç möeç'-te shoo'-e zeh'-en.

A pair of black (brown) shoes.
Ein Paar schwarze (braune) Schuhe.
In pahr shvahrts'-e (brown'-e) shoo'-e.

Try this pair on.
Probieren Sie dieses Paar an.
Proh-beer'-en zee deez'-es pahr ahn.

They are too narrow.
Sie sind zu eng.
Zee zint tsoo ehng.

They are too tight (loose).
Sie sind zu knapp (weit).
Zee zint tsoo knahp (vit).

They are not big enough.
Sie sind nicht gross genug.
Zee zint niçt grohs ge-nookh'.

They are too long (short).
Sie sind zu lang (kurz).
Zee zint tsoo lahng (kurts).

Do you sell cigarettes?
Verkaufen Sie Zigaretten?
Fer-kowf'-en zee tsee-gah-ret'-en?

Do you have matches?
Haben Sie Streichhölzer?
Hahb'-en zee shtriç'-hœlts-er?

I want to buy needles, pins, and some thread.
Ich will Nadeln, Stecknadeln und etwas Faden kaufen.
Iç vil nahd'-eln, shtek'-nahd-eln unt et'-vahs fahd'-en kowf'-en.

How many do you want?
Wieviele wollen Sie?
Vee-feel'-e vol'-en zee?

Anything else?
Noch etwas? / Etwas weiteres?
Nokh et'-vahs? / Et'-vahs vit'-er-es?

No, thank you. That's all.
Nein, danke. Das ist alles.
Nin, dahnk'-e. Dahs ist ahl'-es.

I'll take it (them) with me.
Ich werde es (sie) mitnehmen.
Iç verd'-e es (zee) mit'-nehm-en.

Will you wrap it, please?
Wollen Sie es einpacken, bitte?
Vol'-en zee es in'-pahk-en, bit'-e?

Send it to the hotel.
Schicken Sie es zum Hotel.
Shik'-en zee es tsum hoh-tel'.

Pack it (them) for shipment to . . .
Packen Sie es (sie) ein für Sendung nach . . .
Pahk'-en zee es (zee) in feûr zend'-oong nahkh . . .

Here is the bill.
Hier ist die Rechnung.
Heer ist dee reç'-noong.

I will pay cash.
Ich werde bar zahlen.
Iç verd'-e bahr tsahl'-en.

Is there a discount?
Gibt es einen Abzug?
Geept es in'-en ahp'-tsook?

CLOTHING SIZE CONVERSIONS: *Women*

Dresses, Suits and Coats

American:	8	10	12	14	16	18
British:	30	32	34	36	38	40
Continental:	36	38	40	42	44	46

Blouses and Sweaters

American:	32	34	36	38	40	42	44
British:	34	36	38	40	42	44	46
Continental:	40	42	44	46	48	50	52

Stockings

American and British:	8	8½	9	9½	10	10½	11
Continental:	35	36	37	38	39	40	41

Shoes

American:	5	5½	6	6½	7	7½	8	8½	9
British:	3½	4	4½	5	5½	6	6½	7	7½
Continental:	35	35	36	37	38	38	38½	39	40

Gloves
American, British and Continental sizes are the same.

CLOTHING SIZE CONVERSIONS: *Men*

Suits, Sweaters and Overcoats

American and British:	34	36	38	40	42	44	46	48
Continental:	44	46	48	50	52	54	56	58

Shirts

American and British:	14	14½	15	15½	16	16½	17	17½
Continental:	36	37	38	39	40	41	42	43

Socks

American and British:	9½	10	10½	11	11½	12	12½
Continental:	39	40	41	42	43	44	45

Shoes

American:	7	7½	8	8½	9	9½	10	10½	11	11½
British:	6½	7	7½	8	8½	9	9½	10	10½	11
Continental:	39	40	41	42	43	43	44	44	45	45

Getting Around by Automobile

Since few attendants who work at garages and stations speak English, some ability in German will be very useful. You will need gasoline, of course, and probably some regular servicing. And should there be some problem with the car, a lot of time and energy will be saved if you can explain your needs.

I would like to hire a car.
Ich möchte ein Auto mieten.
Iç möéç'-te in ow'-toh meet'-en.

How much does a car cost per day?
Was kostet ein Auto pro Tag?
Vahs kost'-et in ow'-toh proh tahkh?

How much per kilometer?
Wieviel pro Kilometer?
Vee-feel' proh kee-loh-meht'-er?

Is gasoline expensive in this country?
Is Benzin teuer in diesem Land?
Ist ben-tseen' toy'-er in deez'-em lahnt?

Is there a deposit?
Is eine Anzahlung zu machen?
Ist in'-e ahn'-tsahl-oong tsoo mahkh'-en?

I would like a car with seatbelts and an outside mirror.
Ich möchte einen Wagen mit Sicherheitsgurten und einem
äusseren Spiegel.
*Ic möec'-te in'-en vahg'-en mit ziç'-er-hits-goort-en unt in'-
em oys'-er-en shpeeg'-el.*

I will (will not) take the car out of the country.
Ich werde den Wagen (nicht) aus dem Land nehmen.
Iç verd'-e dehn vahg'-en (niçt) ows dehm lahnt nehm'-en.

I want to leave it in . . .
Ich will ihn in . . . lassen.
Iç vil een in . . . lahs'-en.

How much is the insurance per day?
Was kostet die Versicherung pro Tag?
Vahs kost'-et dee fer-ziç'-er-oong proh tahkh?

Here is the registration and the key.
Hier ist die Eintragung und der Schlüssel.
Heer ist dee in'-trahg-oong unt dehr shlêûs'-el.

Where is there a gas station?   a garage?
Wo ist eine Tankstelle?   eine Garage?
Voh ist in'-e tahnk'-shtel-e?   in'-e gah-rah'-she?

Fill it up.
Machen Sie den Tank voll.
Mahkh'-en zee dehn tahnk fol.

Premium.
Das beste Benzin.
Dahs best'-e ben-tseen'.

Regular.
Gewöhnliches Benzin.
Ge-vőén'-leeç-es ben-tseen'.

I want twenty liters of gasoline.
Ich will zwanzig Liter Benzin.
Iç vil tsvahn'-tseeç leet'-er ben-tseen'.

I also need some oil.
Ich brauche auch etwas Öl.
Iç browkh'-e owkh et'-vahs őél.

Please put in some water.
Bitte, stellen Sie ein wenig Wasser ein.
Bit'-e, shtel'-en zee in veh'-neeç vahs'-er in.

Wash the car, please.
Waschen Sie den Wagen, bitte.
Vahsh'-en zee dehn vahg'-en, bit'-e.

Please inspect the tires.
Bitte, sehen Sie nach den Reifen.
Bit'-e, zeh'-en see nahkh dehn rif'-en.

Put in some air.
Stellen Sie etwas Luft ein.
Shtel'-en zee et'-vahs luft in.

Is there a mechanic here?
Ist ein Mechaniker hier?
Ist in meh-khah'-neek-er heer?

Can you fix a flat tire?
Können Sie eine Reifenpanne reparieren?
Kőén'-en zee in'-e rif'-en-pah-ne reh-pah-reer'-en?

How long will it take?
Wie lange wird es dauern?
Vee lahng'-e veert es dow'-ern?

Have you a road map?
Haben Sie eine Autokarte?
Hahb'-en zee īn'-e ow'-toh-kahrt-e?

Where does this road go to?
Wohin führt diese Strasse?
Voh-hin' fëurt deez'-e shtrahs'-e?

Is this the road to . . . ?
Ist das die Strasse nach . . . ?
Ist dahs dee shtrahs'-e nahkh . . . ?

Is the road good?
Ist die Strasse gut?
Ist dee shtrahs'-e goot?

A narrow road.
Eine schmale Strasse.
Īn'-e shmahl'-e shtrahs'-e.

A wide road.
Eine breite Strasse.
Īn'-e brīt'-e shtrahs'-e.

A narrow bridge.
Eine schmale Brücke.
Īn'-e schmahl'-e brëuk'-e.

A bad road.
Eine schlechte Strasse. / Ein schlechter Weg.
Īn'-e shleçt'-e shtrahs'-e. / In shleçt'-ter vehkh.

This road is slippery when it's wet.
Diese Strasse is schlüpferig (glatt) bei Nässe.
Deez'-e shtrahs'-e ist shlëupf'-er-eeç (glaht) bī nes'-e.

Is there a speed limit here?
Ist hier eine Geschwindigkeitsbegrenzung?
Ist heer īn'-e ge-shvin'-deeç-kīts-be-grents-oong?

You were driving too fast.
Sie fuhren zu schnell.
Zee foor'-en tsoo shnel.

You must pay the fine.
Sie müssen die Geldstrafe bezahlen.
Zee mẻus'-en dee gelt'-shtrahf-e be-tsahl'-en.

May I leave the car here?
Darf ich den Wagen hier lassen?
Dahrf iç dehn vahg'-en heer lahs'-en?

May I park here?
Darf ich hier parken?
Dahrf iç heer pahrk'-en?

Where is the nearest garage?
Wo ist die nächste Garage?
Woh ist dee neçst'-e gah-rah'-she?

The car isn't running well.
Dieser Wagen läuft nicht gut.
Deez'-er vahg'-en loyft niçt goot.

I don't know what the matter is.
Ich weiss nicht was los ist.
Iç vîs niçt vahs lohs ist.

I have a driver's license.
Ich habe einen Führerschein.
Iç hahb'-e în'-en fẻur'-er- shin.

Please check . . .
Bitte, sehen Sie . . . nach.
Bit'-e, zeh'-en zee . . . nahkh.

Can you fix it?
Können Sie es reparieren?
Kẻen'-en zee es reh-pah-reer'-en?

How long will it take?
Wie lange wird es dauern?
Vee lahng'-e veert es dow'- ern?

I think it's . . .	**Is it . . . ?**
Ich glaube, es ist . . .	Ist es . . . ?
Iç glowb'-e, es ist . . .	*Ist est . . . ?*

the accelerator.
das Gaspedal.
dahs gahs'-peh-dahl.

the air filter.
der Luftfilter.
dehr Luft'-filt-er.

the battery.
der Akkumulator / die Batterie.
dehr ah-ku-mu-lah'-tohr / dee bah-te-ree'.

the brakes.
die Bremsen.
dee bremz'-en.

the carburetor.
der Vergaser.
dehr fer-gahz'-er.

the clutch.
die Kuppelung.
die kup'-el-oong.

the lights.
die Scheinwerfer.
dee shin'-verf-er.

the motor.
der Motor.
dehr moh-tohr'.

the spark plugs.
die Zündkerzen.
dee tseūnt'-kerts-en.

the tires.
die Reifen.
dee rif'-en.

the wheel.
das Rad.
dahs raht.

the wheels.
die Räder.
dee rehd'-er.

the front wheel.
das Vorderrad.
dahs for'-der-raht.

the back wheel.
das hintere Rad.
dahs hin'-ter-e raht.

Your car is ready.
Ihr Wagen ist fertig.
Eer vahg'-en ist fer'-teeç.

Drive carefully!
Fahren Sie mit Vorsicht!
Fahr'-en zee mit for'-siçt!

Please wipe the windshield.
Bitte, wischen Sie die Windschutzscheibe.
Bit'-e, vish'-en zee dee vint'-shuts-shīb-e.

Priority road ahead

Some International Road Signs

 = RED

 = BLUE

= BLACK

Stop

Dangerous curve

Right curve

Double curve

Intersection

Intersection with secondary road

Railroad crossing
with gates

Railroad crossing
without gates

Road work

Pedestrian
crossing

Children

Road narrows

Uneven road

Slippery road

Traffic circle
ahead

Danger

Closed to
all vehicles

No entry

No left turn

No U turn

Overtaking
prohibited

Speed limit

Customs

No parking

Direction to
be followed

Traffic circle

No parking

Getting Around by Train

The railroad is the most frequently used means of transportation by visitors abroad. Schedules and timetables are usually readily understandable — if they are visible — but otherwise, in arranging your travel by train, you will need to use some of these phrases.

The railroad station.
Der Bahnhof.
Dehr bahn'-hohf.

The train.
Der Zug.
Dehr tsook.

Drive to the railroad station.
Fahren Sie zum Bahnhof.
Fahr'-en zee tsum bahn'-hohf.

I need a porter.
Ich brauche einen Gepäckträger.
Iç browkh'-e in'-en ge-pek'-trehg-er.

Porter, here is my luggage.
Gepäckträger, hier ist mein Gepäck.
Ge-pek'-trehg-er, heer ist min ge-pek'.

These are my bags.
Das sind meine Handkoffer.
Dahs zint min'-e hahnt'-kof-er.

Here are the baggage checks.
Hier sind die Gepäckscheine.
Heer zint dee ge-pek'-shīn-e.

Where is the ticket window?
Wo is der Fahrkartenschalter?
Voh ist dehr' fahr'-kahrt-en-shahlt-er?

Have you a timetable?
Haben Sie einen Fahrplan?
Hahb'-en zee in'-en fahr'-plahn?

When does the train leave?
Wann fährt der Zug ab?
Vahn fehrt dehr tsook ahp?

From which platform?
Von welchem Bahnsteig?
Fon velç'-em bahn'-shtik?

I want to check this baggage.
Ich will dieses Gepäk aufgeben.
Iç vil deez'-es ge-pek' owf'-gehb-en.

I must pick up a ticket.
Ich muss eine Fahrkarte lösen.
Iç mus in'-e fahr'-kahrt-e lŏèz'-en.

I want a ticket to . . .
Ich will eine Fahrkarte nach . . .
Iç vil in'-e fahr'-kahrt-e nahkh . . .

First class.
Erste Klasse.
Ehrst'-e klahs'-e.

Second class.
Zweite Klasse.
Tsvit'-e klahs'-e.

one way.
Hinfahrt.
Hin'-fahrt.

Round trip.
Hin- und Rückfahrt.
Hin unt rêûk'-fahrt.

Is there a dining car?
Gibt es einen Speisewagen?
Geept es in'-en shpi'-ze-vahg-en?

Does this train go to . . . ?
Fährt dieser Zug nach . . . ?
Fehrt deez'-er tsook nahkh . . . ?

Does this train stop at . . . ?
Hält dieser Zug in . . . ?
Helt deez'-er tsook in . . . ?

Is this train late?
Hat der Zug Verspätung?
Haht dehr tsook fer-shpeht'-oong?

Is this seat occupied?
Is dieser Platz bestzt?
Ist deez'-er plahts be-zetst'?

What is the name of this station?
Wie heisst dieser Bahnhof?
Vee hist deez'-er bahn'-hohf?

How long do we stop here?
Wie lange halten wir hier?
Vee lahng'-e hahlt'-en veer heer?

May I open the window?
Darf ich das Fenster öffnen?
Dahrf iç dahs fens'-ter ôêf'-nen?

Please close the door.
Bitte, machen Sie die Tür zu.
Bit'-e, mahkh'-en zee dee têûr tsoo.

I have missed the train!
Ich habe den Zug verpasst!
Iç hahb'-e dehn tsook fer-pahst'!

When does the next train leave?
Wann fährt der nächste Zug ab?
Vahn fehrt dehr neçst'-e tsook ahp?

Where is the waiting room?
Wo ist der Wartesaal?
Voh ist dehr vahrt'-e-zahl?

Where is the lavatory?
Wo ist die Toilette?
Voh ist dee toy-let'-e?

The train is arriving now.
Der Zug kommt jetzt an.
Dehr tsook komt yetst ahn.

Tickets, please.
Fahrkarten, bitte.
Fahr'-kahrt-en, bit'-e.

All aboard!
Alle einsteigen!
Ahl'-e in'-shtig-en!

The train is leaving.
Der Zug fährt ab.
Dehr tsook fehrt ahp.

Arrivals.
Ankünfte.
Ahn'-keûnft-e.

Departures.
Abreisen. Abfahrten.
Ahp'-riz-en. Ahp'-fahrt-en.

Express train.
Schnellzug.
Shnel'-tsook.

Local train.
Personenzug.
Per-zohn'-en-tsook.

Getting Around by Ship and Plane

If you go abroad on a ship or airplane, your first chance to use your German will come in transit. Being able to speak with the personnel can be an exciting start to a journey. They will be more helpful, too, if you make an effort to speak to them in their language. And your efforts will be rewarded.

There's the harbor (the port).
Da ist der Hafen.
Dah ist dehr hahf'-en.

Where is the pier?
Wo ist der Pier?
Voh ist dehr peer?

When does the ship sail?
Wann fährt das Schiff ab?
Vahn fehrt dahs shif ahp?

Let's go on board!
Gehen wir an Bord!
Geh'-en veer ahn bort!

Where is cabin number . . . ?
Wo ist Kabine Nummer . . . ?
Voh ist kah-bee'-ne num'-er . . . ?

Is this my cabin (stateroom)?
Ist dies meine Kabine?
Ist dees mīn'-e kah-bee'-ne?

Steward, do you have the key to my cabin?
Steward, haben Sie den Schlüssel für meine Kabine?
Shtoo'-ahrt, hahb'-en zee dehn shlĕûs'-el fĕûr mīn'-e kah-bee'-ne?

I'm looking for the dining room.
Ich suche den Speisesaal.
Iç zookh'-e dehn shpī'-ze-zahl.

We want a table for two.
Wir möchten einen Tisch für zwei haben.
Veer mȫç'-ten īn'-en tish fĕûr tsvī hahb'-en.

A first-class cabin.
Eine erstklassige Kabine.
Īn'-e ehrst'-klahs-ee-ge kah-bee'-ne.

A second-class cabin.
Eine zweitklassige Kabine.
Īn'-e tsvīt'-klahs-ee-ge kah-bee'-ne.

Let's go on deck.
Gehen wir aufs Deck.
Geh'-en veer owfs dek.

I would like a deck chair.
Ich möchte einen Liegestuhl haben.
Iç mȫç'-te īn'-en lee'-ge-shtool hahb'-en.

I would like to eat by the swimming pool.
Ich möchte beim Schwimmbad essen.
Iç mȫç'-te bīm shvim'-baht es'-en.

The ship arrives at seven o'clock.
Das Schiff kommt um sieben Uhr an.
Dahs shif komt um zee'-ben oor ahn.

When do we go ashore?
Wann gehen wir an Land?
Vahn geh'-en veer ahn lahnt?

Where is the gangplank?
Wo ist der Landungssteg?
Voh ist dehr lahnd'-oongs-shtehk?

The landing card, please.
Die Landungskarte, bitte.
Dee lahnd'-oongs-kahrt-e, bit'-e.

I wasn't seasick at all!
Ich war gar nicht seekrank!
Iç vahr gahr niçt zeh'-krahnk!

Have a good trip!
Gute Reise!
Goot'-e riz'-e!

I want to go to the airport.
Ich will zum Flughafen fahren.
Iç vil tsum flook'-hahf-en fahr'-en.

Drive me to the airport.
Fahren Sie mich zum Flughafen.
Fahr'-en zee miç tsum flook'-hahf-en.

When does the plane leave?
Wann fliegt das Flugzeug ab?
Vahn fleekt dahs flook'-tsoyk ahp?

When does it arrive?
Wann kommt es an?
Vahn komt es ahn?

Flight number . . . leaves at six o'clock.
Flug Nummer . . . fliegt um sechs Uhr ab.
Flook num'-er . . . fleekt um zeks oor ahp.

From which gate?
Von welcher Pforte?
Fon velç'-er pfort'-e?

I want to reconfirm my flight.
Ich will meinen Flug wieder bestätigen.
Iç vil min'-en flook veed'-er be-shteht'-ee-gen.

Ticket, please.
Fahrkarte, bitte.
Fahr'-kahrt-e, bit'-e.

Boarding pass, please.
Besteigungspass, bitte.
Be-shti'-goongs-pahs, bit'-e.

Please fasten your seat belts.
Bitte, anschnallen.
Bit'-e, ahn'-shnahl-en.

No smoking.
Nicht rauchen.
Niçt rowkh'-en.

Stewardess, a small pillow, please.
Stewardess, einen kleinen Kopfkissen, bitte.
Shtoo'-ahrd-es, in'-en klin'-en kopf'-kis-en, bit'-e.

I fly to Europe every year.
Ich fliege jedes Jahr nach Europa.
Iç fleeg'-e yehd'-es yahr nahkh oy-roh'-pah.

The airplane is taking off!
Das Flugzeug startet!
Dahs flook'-tsoyk shtahrt'-et!

Is a meal served during this flight?
Wird eine Mahlzeit während dieses Fluges serviert?
Veert in'-e mahl'-tsit veh'-rent deez'-es floog'-es ser-veert'?

The airplane will land in ten minutes.
Das Flugzeug wird binnen zehn Minuten landen.
Dahs flook'-tsoyk veert bin'-en tsehn mee-noot'-en lahnd'-en.

There will be a delay.
Wir haben Verspätung.
Veer hahb'-en fer-shpeht'-oong.

There's the runway!
Da ist die Rollbahn!
Dah ist dee rol'-bahn!

We have arrived!
Wir sind angekommen!
Veer zint ahn'-ge-kom-en!

Health

We hope you will never need the phrases you will find
in this section; but emergencies do arise, and sickness does
overwhelm. Since a physician's diagnosis often depends
on what you, the patient, can tell him, you will want to
make your woes clearly understood. If you have a chronic
medical problem, you might well arrange to have various
prescriptions or descriptions of the difficulty in hand or
translated before you leave on your trip.

I need a doctor.
Ich brauche einen Arzt.
Iç browkh'-e in'-en ahrtst.

Send for a doctor.
Lassen Sie einen Arzt kommen.
Lahs'-en zee in'-en ahrtst kom'-en.

Are you the doctor?
Sind Sie der Arzt?
Zint zee dehr ahrtst?

What is the matter with you?
Was fehlt Ihnen?
Vahs fehlt ee'-nen?

I don't feel well.
Ich fühle mich nicht wohl.
Iç féûl'-e miç niçt vohl.

I am sick.
Ich bin krank.
Iç bin krahnk.

How long have you been sick?
Seit wann sind Sie krank?
Zīt vahn zint zee krahnk?

I have a headache.
Ich habe Kopfschmerzen.
Iç hahb'-e kopf'-shmerts-en.

the arm, the arms der Arm, die Arme *dehr ahrm, dee ahrm'-e*	**the back** der Rücken *dehr rēûk'-en*
the bladder die Harnblase *dee hahrn'-blahz-e*	**the bone** der Knochen *dehr knokh'-en*
the chest die Brust *dee brust*	**the ear, the ears** das Ohr, die Ohren *dahs ohr, dee ohr'-en*
the elbow der Ellbogen *dehr el'-bohg-en*	**the eye, the eyes** das Auge, die Augen *dahs ow'-ge, dee ow'-gen*
the face das Gesicht *dahs ge-ziçt'*	**the finger** der Finger *dehr feeng'-er*
the foot, the feet der Fuss, die Füsse *dehr foos, dee fēûs'-e*	**the forehead** die Stirn *dee shteern*

Where is the hospital?
Wo ist das Krankenhaus?
Voh ist dahs krahnk'-en-hows?

Is there a drugstore near here?
Ist eine Apotheke hier in der Nähe?
Ist in'-e ah-poh-teh'-ke heer in dehr neh'-e?

I have a stomach ache.
Ich habe Magenschmerzen.
Iç hahb'-e mahg'-en-shmerts-en.

Where does it hu...
Wo schmerzt es?
Voh shmertst es?

the hair das Haar, die Haare *dahs hahr, dee hahr'-e*	**my hair** mein Haar, meine Haare *min hahr, min'-e hahr'-e*
the hand, the hands die Hand, die Hände *dee hahnt, dee hend'-e*	**the head** der Kopf *dehr kopf*
the heart das Herz *dahs herts*	**the hip** die Hüfte *dee hüft'-e*
the joint das Gelenk *dahs ge-lehnk'*	**the kidneys** die Nieren *dee neer'-en*
the knee das Knie *dahs knee*	**the leg, the legs** das Bein, die Beine *dahs bin, dee bin'-e*
the liver die Leber *dee lehb'-er*	**the lung, the lungs** die Lunge, die Lungen *dee lung'-e, dee lung'-en*
the mouth der Mund *dehr munt*	**the muscle** der Muskel *dehr musk'-el*

...s.	**My finger is bleeding.**
...n schmerzt.	Mein Finger blutet.
	Min feeng'-er bloot'-et.
...I have a fever?	**I have burned myself.**
Habe ich Fieber?	Ich habe mich verbrannt.
Hahb'-e iç feeb'-er?	*Iç hahb'-e miç fer-brahnt'.*
You must stay in bed.	**How long?**
Sie müssen im Bett bleiben.	Wie lange?
Zee mêus'-en im bet blib'-en.	*Vee lahng'-e?*

---

the neck	**the nose**
der Hals	die Nase
dehr hahlss	*dee nahz'-e*
the shoulder	**the skin**
die Schulter	die Haut
dee shult'-er	*dee howt*
the skull	**the spine**
der Schädel	das Rückgrat
dehr sheh'-del	*dahs rêuk'-graht*
the stomach	**the thigh**
der Magen	der Schenkel
dehr mahg'-en	*dehr shehnk'-el*
the throat	**the thumb**
die Kehle	der Daumen
dee keh'-le	*dehr dowm'-en*
the toe	**the tooth, the teeth**
die Zehe	der Zahn, die Zähne
dee tseh'-e	*dehr tsahn, dee tsehn'-e*
the waist	**the wrist**
die Taille	das Handgelenk
dee tahl'-ye	*dahs hant'-ge-lehnk*

At least two days.
Am wenigstens zwei Tage.
Ahm veh'-neeks-tens tsvi tahg'-e.

Show me your tongue.
Zeigen Sie mir die Zunge.
Tsig'-en zee meer dee tsung'-e.

Lie down.
Legen Sie sich hin.
Lehg'-en zee ziç hin.

Get up.
Stehen Sie auf.
Shteh'-en zee owf.

I have a cold.
Ich habe eine Erkältung.
Iç hahb'-e in'-e ehr-kelt'-oong.

Do you smoke?
Rauchen Sie?
Rowkh'-en zee?

Yes, I smoke.
Ja, ich rauche.
Yah, iç rowkh'-e.

No, I don't smoke.
Nein, ich rauche nicht.
Nin, iç rowkh'-e niçt.

Do you sleep well?
Schlafen Sie gut?
Shlahf'-en zee goot?

No, I don't sleep well.
Nein, ich schlafe nicht gut.
Nin, iç shlahf'-e niçt goot.

Take this medicine three times a day.
Nehmen Sie diese Arznei dreimal im Tag.
Nehm'-en zee deez'-e ahrts-ni' dri'-mahl im tahkh.

I cough frequently.
Ich huste häufig.
Iç hoost'-e hoy'-feeç.

Here is a prescription.
Hier ist ein Rezept.
Heer ist in reh-tsept'.

Can you come again tomorrow?
Können Sie morgen wiederkommen?
Köen'-en zee mor'-gen veed'-er-kom-en?

Yes, I can come.
Ja, ich kann kommen.
Yah, iç kahn kom'-en.

I will come later.
Ich werde später kommen.
Iç verd'-e shpeht'-er kom'-en.

He's a good doctor.
Er ist ein guter Arzt.
Ehr ist in goot'-er ahrtst.

Sightseeing

No phrase book can possibly supply you with all the phrases you might want in the infinite number of situations, emotions, likes, and dislikes you will encounter in your travels. The basics are here, but they can only be a beginning. The dictionary at the back of this book will supply you with a larger vocabulary to use with the phrases. In addition, local bilingual or multilingual guides are usually very helpful in supplying other language information concerning a given situation. If an unusual phrase is required, ask him and it will be given to you gladly.

I would like to go sightseeing.
Ich möchte die besuchen Sehenswürdigkeiten.
Iç möeç'-te dee be-zookh'-en zeh'-ens-vēurd-eeç-kit-en.

How long does the tour last?
Wie lange dauert die Rundfahrt?
Vee lahng'-e dow'-ert dee runt'-fahrt?

It last three hours.
Sie dauert drei Stunden.
Zee dow'-ert dri shtund'-en.

Are you the guide?
Sind Sie der Reiseleiter?
Zint zee dehr riz'-e-lit-er?

What is the name of this place?
Wie heisst dieser Platz?
Vee hist deez'-er plahts?

Are the museums open today?
Sind die Museen heute geöffnet?
Zint dee moo-zeh'-en hoy'-te ge-ŏef'-net?

No, the museums are closed today.
Nein, die Museen sind heute geschlossen.
Nin, dee moo-zeh'-en zint hoy'-te ge-shlos'-en.

The stores are open.
Die Kaufläden (Geschäfte) sind geöffnet.
Dee kowf'-lehd-en (ge-sheft'-e) zint ge-ŏef'-net.

I would like to visit an art museum.
Ich möchte ein Kunstmuseum besuchen.
Iç mŏeç'-te in kunst'-moo-zeh-oom be-zookh'-en.

Is there an exhibition there now?
Gibt es dort jetzt eine Ausstellung?
Geept es dort yetst in'-e ows'-shtel-oong?

I would like to see the city.
Ich möchte die Stadt besichtigen.
Iç mŏeç'-te dee shtaht be-ziç'-tee-gen.

What is the name of that church?
Wie heisst jene Kirche?
Vee hist yehn'-e keerç'-e?

May we go in?
Dürfen wir eintreten?
Deûrf'-en veer in'-treht-en?

Is the old church closed this morning?
Ist die alte Kirche heute morgen geschlossen?
Ist dee ahlt'-e keerç'-e hoy'-te mor'-gen ge-shlos'-en?

Will it be open this evening?
Wird sie heute abend geöffnet sein?
Veert zee hoy'-te ah'-bent ge-öef'-net zin?

This is the main square of the city.
Das ist der Hauptplatz der Stadt.
Dahs ist dehr howpt'-plahts dehr shtaht.

May I take pictures here?
Darf ich hier Aufnahmen machen?
Dahrf iç heer owf'-nahm-en mahkh'-en?

We have walked a lot.
Wir haben viel spaziert.
Veer hahb'-en feel shpah-tseert'.

I am tired.
Ich bin müde.
Iç bin meû'-de.

Let's sit down.
Setzen wir uns.
Zets'-en veer uns.

Where does this street lead to?
Wohin führt diese Strasse?
Voh-hin' feûrt deez'-e shtrahs'-e?

To the cathedral.
Zum Dom.
Tsum dohm.

What is that monument?
Was ist das Denkmal?
Vahs ist dahs dehnk'-mahl?

Is that a theater?
Ist das ein Theater?
Ist dahs in teh-ah'-ter?

It's a movie house.
Es ist ein Kino.
Es ist in kee'-noh.

What is the name of this park?
Wie heisst dieser Park?
Vee hist deez'-er pahrk?

We cross the street here.
Wir gehen hier die Strasse hinüber.
Veer geh'-en heer dee shtrahs'-e hin-êub'-er.

Will we visit a castle?
Werden wir ein Schloss besuchen?
Verd'-en veer in shlos be-zookh'-en?

We will visit a palace.
Wir werden einen Palast besuchen.
Veer verd'-en in'-en pah-lahst' be-zookh'-en.

Who lives in this palace?
Wer wohnt in diesem Palast?
Vehr vohnt in deez'-em pah-lahst'?

Nobody lives here.
Niemand wohnt hier.
Nee'-mahnt vohnt heer.

What is the name of this river?
Wie heisst dieser Fluss?
Vee hist deez'-er flus?

This is the longest bridge in the city.
Das ist die längste Brücke der Stadt.
Dahs ist dee lehngst'-e brêuk'-e dehr shtaht.

There's too much water in the boat.
Es gibt zu viel Wasser im Boot.
Es geept tsoo feel vahs'-er im boht.

Is our hotel near the river?
Ist unser Hotel in der Nähe des Flusses?
Ist unz'-er hoh-tel' in dehr neh'-e des flus'-es?

This is the shopping center.
Das ist das Kaufzentrum.
Dahs ist dahs kowf'-tsen-troom.

Is it far from here to the beach?
Ist es weit von hier zum Strand?
Ist es vit fon heer tsum shtrahnt?

I would like to go swimming this morning.
Ich möchte heute morgen schwimmen gehen.
Iç möeç'-te hoy'-te mor'-gen shvim'-en geh'-en.

If it doesn't rain, we'll go there.
Wenn es nicht regnet, werden wir dorthin gehen.
Ven es niçt rehg'-net, verd'-en veer dort-hin' geh'-en.

Thank you for an interesting tour.
Ich danke Ihnen für eine interessante Rundfahrt.
Iç dahnk'-e ee'-nen füür in'-e in-te-re-sahnt'-e runt'-fahrt.

Thank you very much for it.
Danke vielmals dafür.
Dahnk'-e feel'-mahlss dah-füür'.

I like it.
Sie gefällt mir.
Zee ge-felt' meer.

I liked it.
Sie ist mir gefallen.
Zee ist meer ge-fahl'-en.

DICTIONARY

Some Tips on German Grammar

Gender Nouns in German are masculine (m), feminine (f), or neuter (n). This is important to know, since the form of other parts of speech (definite and indefinite articles, adjectives, pronouns) depend on whether they modify or appear in connection with a masculine, feminine, or neuter noun. The definite and indefinite articles (the, a, an) and adjectives always agree with the noun in number and gender. The definite article (the) is *der* for masculine singular nouns in the nominative case, *die* for feminine singular nouns, and *das* for neuter singular nouns. In the nominative plural, all genders take the definite article *die*. The indefinite article (a, an) is *ein*, *eine*, and *ein* for masculine, feminine, and neuter, respectively. Notice the following:

> *ein langer Fluss*, a long river (masculine)
> *lange Flüsse*, long rivers
> *der lange Fluss*, the long river
> *die langen Flüsse*, the long rivers
> *eine lange Strasse*, a long street (feminine)
> *lange Strassen*, long streets
> *die lange Strasse*, the long street
> *die langen Strassen*, the long streets
> *ein langes Feld*, a long field (neuter)
> *lange Felder*, long fields
> *das lange Feld*, the long field
> *die langen Felder*, the long fields

Plurals German nouns (which are always capitalized) form their plurals in a variety of ways. Notice the following:

Mann, man	*Männer*, men
Frau, woman	*Frauen*, women
Messer, knife	*Messer*, knives
Apfel, apple	*Äpfel*, apples
Küche, kitchen	*Küchen*, kitchens
Hund, dog	*Hunde*, dogs
Hand, hand	*Hände*, hands

No general guide to the formation of plurals can be given. They must be learned as one's vocabulary grows.

Case Nouns, pronouns, adjectives, and articles have four cases indicating the use of the word in a sentence. They are nominative (subject), genitive (possessive), dative (indirect object), and accusative (direct object).

Verbs Person is indicated in verbs by the use of the personal pronoun before the verb and an ending attached to the verb stem. The verb stem is got by dropping the *-en* or *-n* from the infinitive. Notice the following:

> *trinken,* to drink
> *ich trinke,* I drink
> *er trinkt,* he drinks
> *wir trinken,* we drink
> *sie trinken,* they drink
>
> *sprechen,* to speak
> *ich spreche,* I speak
> *er spricht,* he speaks
> *wir sprechen,* we speak
> *sie sprechen,* they speak
>
> *essen,* to eat
> *ich esse,* I eat
> *sie isst,* she eats
> *wir essen,* we eat
> *sie essen,* they eat

a, ein, eine *in, in'-e*

able, fähig *feh'-eeç;* [to be able], können *kœn-en*

aboard, an Bord *ahn bort*

about *adv.,* ungefähr *un-ge-fehr'*

about *prep.,* über *êu'-ber*

above, über *êu'-ber*

abroad, im Ausland, ins Ausland *im ows'-lahnt, ins ows'-lahnt*

absolutely, absolut *ahp-soh-loot'*

accelerate, beschleunigen *be-shloy'-neeg-en*

accelerator, Gaspedal (n) *gahs'-peh-dahl*

accent *n.,* Akzent (m) *ahk-tsent'*

accept, annehmen *ahn'-nehm-en* [30]

accident, Unfall (m) *un'-fahl* [13]

according to, nach *nahkh*

acount *n.,* Rechnung (f) *reç'-noong*

ache *n.,* Schmerz (m) *shmerts*

ache *v.,* schmerzen *shmerts'-en*

acquaintance, Bekannte (m, f), Bekanntschaft (f) *be-kahnt'-e, be-kahnt'-shahft*

across, gegenüber, über *geh-gen-êu'-ber, êu'-ber*

act *n.,* Tat (f) *taht*

act [do], sich benehmen *ziç be-nehm'-en;* [perform], darstellen *dahr'-shtel-en*

active, tätig *teht'-eeç*

actor, Schauspieler (m) *show'-shpeel-er*

actress, Schauspielerin (f) *show'-shpeel-er-in*

actual, wirklich *veerk'-leeç*

add, hinzufügen *hin-tsoo'-fêug-en*

address *n.,* Adresse (f), Anschrift (f) *ah-dres'-e, ahn'-shrift* [29]

admiration, Bewunderung (f) *be-vund'-er-oong*

admire, bewundern *be-vund'-ern*

admission, Zutritt (m) *tsoo'-trit*

admit, zugeben, gestehen, herein lassen *tsoo'-gehb-en, ge-shteh'-en, her-in lahs'-en*

adorable, entzückend *ent-tseûk'-ent*

advance *v.*, vorrücken, vordringen *for'-reûk-en, for'-dreeng-en*

advantage, Vorteil (m) *for'-til*

adventure, Abenteuer (n) *ah'-ben-toy-er*

advertisement, Anzeige (f), Reklame (f) *ahn'-tsig-e, reh'-klahm'-e*

advice, Rat (m) *raht*

advise, raten *raht'-en*

affectionate, zärtlich *tsert'-leeç*

afraid *adj.*, ängstlich, bange *engst'-leeç, bahng'-e*; [to be afraid], Angst haben, sich fürchten *ahngst hahb'-en, ziç feûrçt'-en*

after, nach *nahkh*

afternoon, Nachmittag (m) *nahkh'-mit-tahkh*

afterwards, nachdem *nahkh-dehm'*

again, wieder *veed'-er*

against, gegen, wider *gehh'-en, veed'-er*

age, Alter (n) *ahlt'-er*

agent, Agent (m), Vertreter (m) *ah-gent', fer'-treht'-er*

ago, vor *for*

agree: to be in accord, übereinstimmen, einverstanden sein *eû-ber-in'-shtim-en, in'-fer-shtahnd-en zin*

agreeable [pleasing], angenehm *ahn'-ge-nehm*

agreement, Übereinstimmung (f) *eû-ber-in'-shtim-oong*

ahead: straight ahead, geradeaus *ge-rah-de-ows'*

air, Luft (f) *luft* [74]

air filter, Luftfilter (m) *luft'-filt-er*

air line, Luftverkehrslinie (f) *luft'-fer-kehrs-leen-ye*

airmail, Flugpost (f) *flook'-post*

airplane, Flugzeug (n) *flook'-tsoyk* [89, 90]

airport, Flughafen (m) *flook'-hahf-en* [44, 89]

alarm, Alarm (m) *ah-lahrm'*

alarm clock, Weckuhr (f) *vek'-oor*

alcohol, Alkohol (m) *ahl'-koh-hohl*

alike, ähnlich, gleich *ehn'-leeç, gliç*

alive, lebendig *leh-ben'-deeç*

all, alle *ahl'-e* **not at all,** gar nicht *gahr niçt* **after all,** doch *dokh*

allergy, Allergie (f) *ah-ler-gee'*

allow, erlauben, gestatten *ehr-lowb'-en, ge-shtaht'-en*

almond, Mandel (f) *mahn'-del*

almost, fast *fahst*

alone, allein *ah-lin'*

along, entlang *ent-lahng'*

already, schon *shohn* [56]

also, auch *owkh*

altar, Altar (m) *ahl-tahr'*

alter, verändern *fer-end'-ern*

alteration [of clothing], Änderung (f) *end'-er-oong*

although, obwohl, obgleich *op-vohl', op-gliç'*

altogether, gänzlich *gents'-leeç*

always, immer, stets *im'-er, shtehts*

am: I am, ich bin *iç bin*

ambassador, Botschafter (m) *boht'-shahft-er*

American, Amerikaner (m), Amerikanerin (f) *ah-meh-ree-kahn'-er, ah-meh-ree-kahn'-er-in*

amount, Betrag (m) *be-trahkh'*

amusement, Unterhaltung (f) *un'-ter-hahlt-oong*

amusing, amüsant, unterhaltend *ah-mêu-zahnt', un'-ter-hahlt-ent*

an, ein, eine *in, in'-e*

and, und *unt*

anger n., Ärger (m), Zorn (m) *ehrg'-er, tsorn*

angry, zornig, böse, ärgerlich *tsorn'-eeç, bôez'-e, ehrg'-er-leeç*

animal, Tier (n) *teer*

ankle, Fussknöchel (m) *foos'-knôekh-el*

announce, ankündigen, melden *ahn'-kêun-dee-gen, meld'-en*

annoy, belästigen *be-les'-tee-gen*

another, ein anderer, eine andere, ein anderes *in ahn'-der-er, in'-e ahn'-der-e, in ahn'der-es*

answer *n.,* Antwort (f) *ahnt'-vort*

answer *v.,* antworten *ahnt'-vort-en* [41]

antique shop, Antiquitätenladen (m) *ahn-tee-kvee-teht'-en-lahd-en*

anxious, besorgt, gespannt *be-zorkt', ge-shpahnt'*

any, irgendwelche *eer'-gent-velç-e*

anybody, irgendeiner, irgendeine *eer'-gent-in-er, eer'-gent-in-e*

anyhow, sowieso, jedenfalls *zoh-vee-zoh', yehd'-en-fahlss*

anything, irgendetwas *eer'-gent-et-vahs*

anywhere, irgendwo *eer'-gent-voh*

apartment, Wohnung (f), Mietshaus (n) *vohn'-oong, meets'-hows*

apologize, sich entschuldigen *siç ent-shul'-dee-gen*

apology, Entschuldigung (f) *ent-shul'-dee-goong*

appear, erscheinen *ehr-shin'-en*

appendicitis, Blinddarmentzündung (f) *blint'-dahrm-ent-tseünd-oong*

appendix, Blinddarm (m) *blint'-dahrm*

appetite, Appetit (m) *ah-peh-teet'*

appetizer, Vorspeise (f) *for'-shpiz-e*

apple, Apfel (m) *ahpf'-el*

appointment, Vereinbarung (f), Verabredung (f) *fer-in'-bahr-oong, fer-ahp'-rehd-oong*

appreciate, schätzen *shets'-en*

approve, genehmigen, billigen *ge-neh'-mee-gen, bil'-ee-gen*

approximately, ungefähr *un-ge-fehr'*

April, April (m) *ah-preel'*

arch, Bogen (m) *bohg'-en*

architect, Architekt (m), Baumeister (m) *ahr-khee-tekt', bow'-mist-er*

architecture, Baukunst (f) *bow'-kunst*

are: you are, Sie sind, du bist *zee zint, doo bist* **you** (pl),
they are, ihr seid, sie sind *eer zit, zee zint* **we are,**
wir sind *veer zint*

area, Gebiet (n) *ge-beet'*

argue, erörtern *ehr-ŏĕrt'-ern*

arm, Arm (m) *ahrm*

around, ringsherum, um *reengs-her-um', um*

arrange, ordnen, anordnen, einrichten *ord'-nen, ahn'-ord-
nen, in'-riçt-en*

arrest *v.,* verhaften *fer-hahft'-en*

arrival, Ankunft (f) *ahn'-kunft* [86]

arrive, ankommen *ahn'-kom-en* [24, 45, 86, 88, 89, 90]

art, Kunst (f) *kunst* [98]

artichoke, Artischocke (f) *ahr-tee-shok'-e*

article, Artikel (m) *ahr-teek'-el*

artificial, künstlich *kĕunst'-leeç*

artist, Künstler (m), Künstlerin (f) *kĕunst'-ler, kĕunst'-
ler-in*

as, wie *vee*

ashamed, sich schämen *ziç shehm'-en*

ashore, an Land *ahn lahnt* [89]

ashtray, Aschenbecher (m) *ah'-shen-beç-er* [50]

ask, fragen *frahg'-en*

asleep, eingeschlafen *in'-ge-shlahf-en*

asparagus, Spargel (m) *shpahrg'-el*

aspirin, Aspirin (n) *Ahs-pee-reen'*

assist, beistehen *bi'-shteh-en*

assistant, Assistent (m), Gehilfe (m), Gehilfin (f) *ah-sees-
tent', ge-hilf'-e, ge-hilf'-in*

associate *n.,* Kollege (m) *ko-leh'-ge*

association, Vereinigung (f) *fer-in'-ee-goong*

assure, versichern *fer-ziç'-ern*

at *prep.,* an, bei, zu *ahn, bi, tsoo*

Atlantic, Atlantik (m) *aht-lahn'-teek*

attach, anhängen *ahn'-hehng-en*

attain, erreichen *ehr-riç'-en*

attempt *v.*, versuchen *fer-zookh'-en*

attend, beiwohnen *bi'-vohn-en*

attention, Aufmerksamkeit (f), Achtung (f) *owf-merk'-zahm-kit, ahkh'-toong*

attract, anziehen *ahn'-tsee-en*

audience, Zuhörerschaft (f), Publikum (n) *tsoo-höer-er-shahft, poob'-lee-kum*

August, August (m) *ow-goost'*

aunt, Tante (f) *tahn'-te*

author, Schriftsteller (m), Verfasser (m) *shrift'-shtel-er, fer-fahs'-er*

authority, Autorität (f) *ow-toh-ree-teht'*

automobile, Automobil (n), Auto (n), Wagen (m) *ow-toh-moh-beel', ow'-toh, vahg'-en*

autumn, Herbst (m) *herpst*

available, verfügbar *fer-feük'-bahr*

avenue, Allee (f) *ah-leh'*

avoid, vermeiden *fer-mid'-en*

await, erwarten *ehr-vahrt'-en*

awake *adj.*, wach *vahkh*

awake *v.*, erwachen *ehr-vahkh'-en*

away, fort, weg *fort, vehkh*

axle, Achse (f) *ahk'-se*

baby, Kindlein (n) *kint'-lin*

bachelor, Junggeselle (m) *yung'-ge-zel-e*

back *adv.*, zurück *tsoo-reük'*

back *n.*, Rücken (m) *reük'-en*

back: to go back, zurückkehren *tsoo-reük'-kehr-en* [12]

bacon, Speck (m) *shpek*

bad, schlecht, schlimm *shleçt, shlim*

badly, schlecht *shleçt*

bag, Sack (m) *zahk*; [suitcase], Handkoffer (m) *hahnt'-kof-er* [33, 84]

baggage, Gepäck (n) *ge-pek'* [84]

baggage check, Gepäckschein (m) *ge-pek'-shin* [84]

bakery, Bäckerei (f) *bek-er-i'*
balcony, Balkon (m) *bahl-kohn'*
ball, Ball (m) *bahl*
banana, Banane (f) *bah-nah'-ne*
band [music], Musikkapelle (f) *moo-zeek'-kah-pel-e*
bandage, Verband (m) *fer-bahnt'*
bank, Bank (f) *bahnk* [29]
bar, Bar (f) *bahr*
barber, Barbier (m), Friseur (m) *bahr-beer', free-zöer'*
bargain *n.*, Gelegenheitskauf (m) *ge-lehg'-en-hits-kowf*
basket, Korb (m) *korp*
bath, Bad (n) *baht* [36]
bathe, baden *bahd'-en*
bathing suit, Badeanzug (m) *bah'-de-ahn-tsook*
bathroom, Badezimmer (n) *bah'-de-tsim-er* [38]
battery, Batterie (f), Akkumulator (m) *bah-te-ree', ah-koo-moo-lah'-tohr*
bay, Bucht (f) *bookht*
be, sein *zin*
beach, Strand (m) *shtrahnt* [101]
beans, Bohnen (f, pl) *bohn'-en*
beard, Bart (m) *bahrt*
beautiful, schön *shöen* [9]
beauty parlor, Schönheitssalon (m) *shöen'-hits-zah-lohn*
because, weil *vil*
become, werden *verd'-en*
bed, Bett (n) *bet* [94]   **to go to bed,** ins Bett gehen *ins bet geh'-en* [24]
bedroom, Schlafzimmer (n) *shlahf'-tsim-er*
bee, Biene (f) *bee'-ne*
beef, Rindfleisch (n) *rint'-flish*
beefsteak, Beefsteak (n) *beef'-shtehk*
beer, Bier (n) *beer* [55]
beet, rote Rübe (f) *roht'-e reüb'-e*
before [time], früher *freü'-er*; [place], vor *for*
begin, anfangen, beginnen *ahn'-fahng-en, be-gin'-en* [5]

beginning, Anfang (m), Beginn (m) *ahn'-fahng, be-gin'*
behind, hinten, hinter *hin'-ten, hin'-ter*
believe, glauben *glowb'-en*
bell, Glocke (f) *glok'-e*
belong, gehören *ge-höer'-en*
belt, Gürtel (m) *geürt'-el*
beside, neben *nehb'-en*
best, beste *best'-e*
better *adj. & adv.,* besser *bes'-er*
between, zwischen *tsvish'-en*
big, gross *grohss* [68]
bill, Rechnung (f) *reç'-noong* [56, 70]
bird, Vogel (m) *fohg'-el*
birth, Geburt (f) *ge-burt'*
birthday, Geburtstag (m) *ge-burts'-tahkh*
bit: a bit, ein bisschen, ein wenig *in bis'-çen, in vehn'-eeç*
bite *v.,* beissen *bis'-en*
black, schwarz, *shvahrts*
blanket, Bettdecke (f) *bet'-dek-e*
bleed, bluten *bloot'-en* [94]
blind, blind *blint*
blister, Blase (f) *blahz'-e*
block *n.,* Klotz (m) *klots*
blonde, blond *blont*
blood, Blut (n) *bloot*
blouse, Bluse (f) *blooz'-e*
blue, blau *blow*
boarding house, Pension (f) *pen-syohn'*
boarding pass, Besteigungspass (m) *be-shtig'-oongs-pahs*
  [90]
boat, Boot (n) *boht* [100]
body, Körper (m) *köerp'-er*
boil *v.,* kochen *kohkh'-en*
bone, Knochen (m) *knokh'-en*
book, Buch (n) *bookh* [41]
bookstore, Buchhandlung *bookh'-hahnt-loong*

booth, Zelle (f) *tsel′-e*
boot, Stiefel (m) *shteef′-el*
border *n.*, Grenze (f) *grents′-e*
born: to be born, geboren sein *ge-bohr′-en zin*
borrow, borgen *borg′-en*
both, beide *bid′-e*
bottle, Flasche (f) *flahsh′-e* [54, 55]
bottle opener, Flaschenöffner (m), Korkzieher (m) *flahsh′-en-öef-ner, kork′-tsee-er* [33]
bottom, Boden (m) *bohd′-en*
box, Schachtel (f), Kasten (m) *shahkht′-el, kahst′-en* [33]
boy, Junge (m), Knabe (m) *yung′-e, knahb′-e*
bracelet, Armband (n) *ahrm′-bahnt*
brake *n*, Bremse (f) *bremz′-e*
brandy, Branntwein (m) *brahnt′-vin*
brassiere, Büstenhalter (m) *beùst′-en-halt-er*
brave, tapfer *tahpf′-er*
bread, Brot (n) *broht*
break *v.*, brechen, zerbrechen *breç′-en, tser-breç′-en*
breakfast, Frühstück (n) *freù′-shteùk* [37, 48, 51]
breast, Brust (f) *brust*
breath, Atem (m) *aht′-em*
breathe, atmen *aht′-men*
bridge, Brücke (f) *breùk′-e* [75, 100]
bright, hell *hel*
bring, bringen *breeng′-en* [50, 53, 54, 55]
broken, zerbrochen *tser-brokh′-en*
brother, Bruder (m) *brood′-er* [2]
brown, braun *brown*
bruise *n.*, Quetschung (f) *kvetch′-oong*
brush *n.*, Bürste (f) *beùrst′-e*
brunette, brünett *breùn-et′*
build *v.*, bauen *bow′-en*
building, Gebäude (n) *ge-boyd′-e*
burn *n.*, Brandwunde (f) *brahnt′-vund-e*
burn *v.*, brennen, verbrennen *bren′-en, fer-bren′-en* [94]

burst v., bersten *berst'-en*
bus, Bus (m) *bus* [14, 45, 46]
business, Geschäft (n) *ge-sheft'*
busy, beschäftigt *be-sheft'-eeçt* [42]
but, aber, sondern *ah'-ber, zon'-dern*
butter, Butter (f) *but'-er* [50, 51]
button, Knopf (m) *knopf*
buy, kaufen *kowf'-en* [65]
by, durch, mit, über *doorç, mit, êü-ber*

cabbage, Kohl (m) *kohl*
cabin, Kabine (f) *kah-bee'-ne* [87, 88]
café, Cafe (n) *kah-feh'*
cake, Kuchen (m) *kookh'-en*
call n., Anruf (m) *ahn'-roof*
call v., rufen *roof'-en* [14]
camera, Kamera (f), Photoapparat (m) *kah'-me-rah, foh'-toh-ah-pah-raht*
can n., Büchse (f) *bêüks'-e*
can: to be able, können *kö̂en-en* **I can**, ich kann *iç kahn*
canal, Kanal (m) *kah-nahl'*
cancel v., absagen, aufheben *ahp'-zahg-en, owf'-hehb-en*
candy, Zuckerwerk (n) *tsuk'-er-verk*
candy store, Zuckerbäckerei (f) *tsuk'-er-bek-er-î*
capital, Hauptstadt (f) *howpt'-shtaht*
car, Wagen (m), Auto (n) *vahg'-en, ow'-toh* [72, 73, 74, 76]
carburetor, Vergaser (m) *fer-gahz'-er*
card, Karte (f) *kahrt'-e* [38]
care n., Sorge (f) *zorg'-e*
care v., sich kümmern, sorgen *ziç kêûm'-ern, zorg'-en*
careful, sorgfältig, vorsichtig *zorg'-felt-eeç, for'-ziçt-eeç*
carpet, Teppich (m) *tep'-eeç*
carrot, Mohrrübe (f) *mohr'-rêûb-e*
carry, tragen *trahg'-en* [34]
cash n., Bargeld (n) *bahr'-gelt*
cash v., einlösen *in'-lö̂ez-en* [30]

cashier, Kassierer (m) *kah-seer'-er* [56]
castle, Schloss (n) *shlos* [100]
cat, Katze (f) *kahts'-e*
catch, fangen *fahng'-en*
cathedral, Dom (m) *dohm* [99]
Catholic, katholisch *kah-toh'-leesh*
catsup, Tomatensosse (f) *toh·maht'-en-zohs-e*
cattle, Vieh (n) *fee*
cauliflower, Blumenkohl (m) *bloom'-en-kohl*
caution, Vorsicht (f) *for'-ziçt*
cave, Höhle (f) *hṓeh'-le*
ceiling, Decke (f) *dek'-e*
celery, Sellerie (f) *zel-e-ree'*
cellar, Keller (m) *kel'-er*
cemetary, Friedhof (m), Kirchhof (m) *freed'-hohf, keerç'-hohf*
center, Zentrum (n), Mittelpunkt (m) *tsen'-troom, mit'-el-punkt*
centimeter, Centimeter (m) *tsen'-tee-meht-er*
century, Jahrhundert (n) *yahr'-hund-ert*
ceremony, Feierlichkeit (f) *fi-er-leeç-kit*
certain, gewiss *ge-vis'*
certainly, gern, gerne *gern, gern'-e*
chair, Stuhl (m) *shtool*
chambermaid, Zimmermädchen (n), Stubenmädchen (n) *tsim'-er-meht-çen, shtoob'-en-meht-çen* [39]
champagne, Sekt (m) *zekt*
chance n., Zufall (m) *tsoo'-fahl*
change [coins], Kleingeld (n) *klin'-gelt* [31]
change v., wechseln, ändern *veks'-eln, end'-ern* [30, 31]
chapel, Kapelle (f) *kah-pel'·e*
charge v., berechnen, anschreiben *be-reç'-nen, ahn'-shrib-en*
charming, reizend *rits'-ent*
chauffeur, Fahrer (m) *fahr'-er*
cheap, billig *bil'-eeç* [66]

check *n.*, Scheck (m) *shek* [30] **traveler's check**, Reise-scheck (m) *riz'-e-shek* [30]

check [one's baggage] *v.*, aufgeben *owf'-gehb-en* [84]

check [inspect], prüfen, nachsehen *prēûf'-en, nahkh'-zeh-en* [76]

cheek, Wange (f), Backe (f) *vahng'-e, bahk'-e*

cheese, Käse (m) *keh'-ze*

cherry, Kirsche (f) *keersh'-e*

chest, Brust (f) *brust*

chicken, Hühnchen (n), Huhn (n) *hēûn'-çen, hoon*

child, Kind (n) *kint*

chin, Kinn (n) *kin*

chocolate, Schokolade (f) *shoh-koh-lah'-de*

choose, wählen *vehl'-en*

chop, Kotelett (n) *kot-let'*

Christmas, Weihnachten (f, pl) *vi'-nahkht-en*

church, Kirche (f) *keerç'-e* [99]

cigar, Zigarre (f) *tsee-gahr'-e*

cigarette, Zigarette (f) *tsee-gah-ret'-e* [33, 68]

cinema, Kino (n) *kee'-noh*

circle, Kreis (m) *kris*

citizen, Bürger (m), Bürgerin (f) *bēûrg'-er, bēûrg'-er-in*

city, Stadt (f) *shtaht* [98, 99, 100]

class, Klasse (f) *klahs'-e* **first class**, erste Klasse, *ehrst'-e klahs'-e* **second class**, zweite-Klasse, *tsvit'-e klahs'-e*

classify, klassifizieren *klah-see-fee-tseer'-en*

clean *adj.*, rein, sauber *rin, zow'-ber* [39, 54, 55]

clean *v.*, reinigen, putzen *rin'-ee-gen, puts'-en*

cleaners, Reinigungsanstalt (f) *rin'-ee-goongs-ahn-shtahlt*

clear, klar *klahr*

climb *v.*, klettern *klet'-ern*

clock, Uhr (f) *oor*

close [near], nahe *nah'-e*

close *v.*, schliessen, zumachen *shlees'-en, tsoo'-mahkh-en* [33, 38, 61, 85]

closed, geschlossen, zu *ge-shlos'-en, tsoo* [98, 99]

closet, Schrank (m) *shrahnk*

cloth, Tuch (n) *tookh*

clothes, Kleider (n, pl) *klīd'-er*

cloud, Wolke (f) *volk'-e* [7]

clutch, [of a car], Kuppelung (f) *kup'-e-loong*

coast, Küste (f) *kêust'-e*

coat [overcoat], Mantel (m), Überzieher (m) *mahnt'-el, êu'-ber-tsee-er*

cockroach, Kakerlak (m) *kahk'-er-lahk*

cocktail, Cocktail (m) *kok'-tehl*

coffee, Kaffee (m) *kah-feh'* [50, 52]

cognac, Kognak (m) *kon'-yahk*

coin, Münze (f) *mêunts'-e* [41]

cold *adj.*, kalt *kahlt* [4, 6, 50, 51]

cold *n.*, Erkältung *er-kel'-toong* [95]

collar, Kragen (m) *krahg'-en*

collect, sammeln *zahm'-eln*

collection, Sammlung *zahm'-loong*

college, Universität (f) *oo-nee-ver-see-teht'*

collide, zusammenstossen *tsoo-zahm'-en-shtohs-en*

color, Farbe (f) *fahrb'-e* [67]

comb, Kamm (m) *kahm*

come, kommen *kom'-en* [12, 95, 96]

comfortable, bequem *be-kvehm'*

company, Gesellschaft (f) *ge-zel'-shahft*

comparison, Vergleich (m) *fer-glīç'*

compartment, Abteil (m) *ahp'-til*

complain, sich beklagen *ziç be-klahg'-en*

complete *adj.*, vollständig *fol'-shtend-eeç*

compliment *n.*, Kompliment (n) *kom-plee-ment'*

concert, Konzert (n) *kon-tsert'*

condition, Zustand (m) *tsoo'-shtahnt*

confuse, verwirren *fer-veer'-en*

congratulation, Glückwunsch (m) *glêuk'-vunsh*

connect, sich verbinden *ziç fer-bind'-en*

consent *v.*, zustimmen *tsoo'-shtim-en*

consider v., überlegen, betrachten *eu'-ber-lehg-en, be-trahkht'-en*

constipated, verstopft *fer-shtopft'*

consul, Konsul (m) *kon'-zool*

consulate, Konsulat (n) *kon-zoo-laht'*

contagious, ansteckend *ahn'-shtek-ent*

contain v., enthalten *ent-hahlt'-en*

contented, zufrieden *tsoo-freed'-en*

continue, fortsetzen, fortfahren *fort'-zets-en, fort'-fahr-en*

contrary, entgegengesetzt, im Gegenteil *ent-gehg'-en-ge-zetst, im gehg'-en-til*

convenient, bequem *be-kvehm'*

conversation, Unterhaltung (f), Gespräch (n) *un-ter-hahlt'-oong, ge-shpreç'*

cook n., Kock (m), Köchin (f) *kokh, köèç'-in*

cook v., kochen *kokh'-en*

cool, kühl *keul* [6]

copy, Kopie (f), Abschrift (f) *ko-pee', ahp'-shrift*

corkscrew, Korkzieher (m) *kork'-tsee-er*

corn, Mais (m) *miss*

corner, Ecke (f) *ek'-e*

correct adj., richtig *riçt'-eeç*

cost n., Kosten (f, pl) *kost'-en*

cost v., kosten *kost'-en* [66, 72]

cotton, Baumwolle (f), Watte (f) *bowm'-vol-e, vaht'-e*

cough n., Husten (m) *hoost'-en*

cough v., husten *hoost'-en* [95]

count v., zählen *tsehl'-en* [31]

country, Land (n) *lahnt* [73]

courage, Mut (m) *moot*

course: main course, Hauptgericht (n) *howpt'-ge-riçt*

court, Gericht (n) *ge-riçt'*

courtyard, Hof (m) *hohf* [36]

cover v., bedecken *be-dek'-en*

cow, Kuh (f) *koo*

crab, Kreps (m), Krabbe (f) *kreps, krahb'-e*

cramp, Krampf (m) *krahmpf*

crazy, verrückt *fer-rêukt'*

cream, Sahne (f), Rahm (m) *zah'-ne, rahm*

cross n., Kreuz (n) *kroyts*

cross v., hinübergehen *hin-êu'-ber-geh-en* [100]

crossing, Überfahrt (f), Kreuzung (f) *êu'-ber-fahrt, kroyts'-oong*

crossroads, Kreuzung (f) *kroyts'-oong*

crowd, Menge (f), Gedränge (n) *mehng'-e, ge-drehng'-e*

cry v., weinen *vin'-en*

cucumber, Gurke (f) *goork'-e*

cup, Tasse (f) *tahs'-e* [52]

curve, Kurve (f) *koor'-ve*

custard, Eierrahm (m) *i'-er-rahm*

customer, Kunde (m) *kund'-e*

customs, Zollamt (n) *tsol'-ahmt*

cut [injury], Schnittwunde (f) *shnit'-vun-de*

cut v., schneiden *shnid'-en*

cutlet, Kotelett (n) *kot-let'*

daily, täglich *tehg'-leeç*

damage v., beschädigen *be-sheh'-dee-gen*

damaged, beschädigt *be-sheh'-deeçt*

damp, feucht *foyçt* [6]

dance n., Tanz (m) *tahnts*

dance v., tanzen *tahnts'-en*

danger, Gefahr (f) *ge-fahr'*

dangerous, gefährlich *ge-fehr'-leeç*

dare v., wagen *vahg-en*

dark, dunkel *dunk'-el*

darkness, Dunkelheit (f) *dunk'-el-hit*

date [time], Datum (n) *daht'-oom;* [appointment], Verabredung *fer-ahp'-reh-doong*

daughter, Tochter (f) *tokht'-er* [2]

day, Tag (m) *tahkh* **per day, a day,** pro Tag *proh tahkh*

dead, tot *toht*

dear [endearment], lieb *leep*

December, Dezember (m) *deh-tsem'-ber*

decide, entscheiden *ent-shid'-en*

deck, Deck (n) *dek* [88]

declare, verzollen *fer-tsol'-en* [32]

deep, tief *teef*

deer, Hirsch (m) *heersh*

delay n., Verzögerung (f), Verspätung (f) *fer-tsö͞e'-ger-oong, fer-shpeht'-oong* [90]

delicious, köstlich *kö͞est'-leeç*

delighted, erfreut *ehr-froyt'*

deliver, liefern *leef'-ern*

dentist, Zahnarzt (m) *tsahn'-ahrtst*

deodorant, Desodorierungsmittel (n) *dehz-oh-doh-reer'-oongs-mit-el*

department store, Warenhaus (n) *vahr'-en-hows*

departure, Abreise (f), Abfahrt (f) *ahp'-rize-e, ahp'-fahrt* [86]

deposit v., einzahlen *in'-tsahl-en* [41]

descend, absteigen *ahp'-shtig-en*

describe, beschreiben *be-shrib'-en*

desert n., Wüste (f) *vêu̇st'-e*

desert v., verlassen *fer-lahs'-en*

desire v., wünschen *vêu̇nsh'-en*

desk, Pult (n) *pult*

dessert, Nachtisch (m) Nachspeise (f) *nahkh'-tish, nahkh'-shpiz-e* [55]

destroy, zerstören *tser-shtö͞er'-en*

detour, Umleitung (f), Umweg (m) *um'-lit-oong, um'-vehkh*

develop, entwickeln *ent-vik'-eln*

dial v., wählen *vehl'-en* [41, 42]

diamond, Diamant (m) *dee-ah-mahnt'*

diaper, Windel (f) *vind'-el*

diarrhea, Durchfall (m) *doorç'-fahl*

dictionary, Wörterbuch (n) *vö͞ert'-er-bookh*

die, sterben *shterb'-en*

difference, Unterschied (m) *un'-ter-sheet*

different, verschieden, anders *fer-sheed'-en, ahnd'-ers*

difficult, schwierig, schwer *shveer'-eeç, shvehr*

dine, speisen *shpīz'-en* [52, 53]

dining car, Speisewagen (m) *shpīz'-e-vahg-en* [85]

dining room, Speisesaal (m), Esszimmer (n) *shpīz'-e-zahl, es'-tsim-er* [37, 88]

dinner, Abendessen (n) *ah'-bent-es-en* [48, 50]

direct, direkt, gerade *dee-rekt', ge-rah'-de*

direction, Richtung (f) *riçt'-oong*

director, Direktor (m) *dee-rek-tohr'*

dirty, schmutzig *shmuts'-eeç* [53]

disappear, verschwinden *fer-shvind'-en*

discount *n.*, Abzug (m) *ahp'-tsook* [70]

discuss, besprechen *be-shpreç'-en*

disease, Krankheit (f) *krahnk'-hīt*

dish, Schüssel (f) Gericht (n) *shêūs'-el, ge-riçt'*

disinfect, desinfizieren *des-in-fee-tseer'-en*

distance, Entfernung *ent-fern'-oong*

district, Bezirk (m) *be-tseerk*

disturb, stören *shtōēr'-en*

divorced, geschieden *ge-sheed'-en*

do, tun, machen *toon, mahkh'-en* **how do you do?** wie befinden Sie sich? *vee be-find'-en zee ziç?*

dock, Dock (n) *dok*

doctor, Arzt (m) *ahrtst* [14, 91, 92, 96]

dog, Hund (m) *hunt*

doll, Puppe (f) *pup'-e*

dollar, Dollar *dol'-ahr* [30]

done, getan, gemacht *ge-tahn', ge-mahkht'*

donkey, Esel (m) *ehz'-el*

door, Tür (f) *tēūr* [85]

dose, Dosis (f) *dohz'-ees*

double, doppelt *dop'-elt*

doubt, zweifeln *tsvīf'-eln* **without doubt,** ohne Zweifel *oh'-ne tsvīf'-el*

down, herunter, hinunter, herab, hinab *hehr-un'-ter, hin-un'-ter, hehr-ahp', hin-ahp'* **to go down,** hinabsteigen *hin-ahp'-shtīg-en*

downtown, Stadtmitte (f), Stadtzentrum (n) *shtaht'-mit-e, shatht'-tsen-troom* [45]

dozen, Dutzend (n) *doots'-ent*

drawer, Schublade (f) *shoop'-lah-de*

dress n., Kleid (n) *klīt* [66, 67]

dress [oneself] v., sich anziehen *ziç ahn'-tsee-en*

dressmaker, Schneiderin (f) *shnīd'-er-in*

drink n., Getränk (n) *ge-trehnk'*

drink v., trinken *treenk'-en*

drive v., fahren *fahr'-en* [44, 75 78, 83]

driver, Fahrer (m) *fahr'-er* [43]

drop v., fallen lassen *fahl'-en lahs'-en*

druggist, Apotheker (m) *ah-poh-tehk'-er*

drugstore, Apotheke (f) *ah-poh-tehk'-e* [93]

drunk, betrunken, besoffen *be-trunk'-en, be-zof'-en*

dry, trocken *trok'-en*

duck, Ente (f) *en'-te*

during, während *veh'-rent*

dust, Staub (m) *shtowp*

duty, Pflicht (f) *pfliçt*; [tax], Zoll (m) *tsol* [33]

dysentery, Ruhr (f) *roor*

each, jeder *yehd'-er*

each one, jeder *yehd'-er*

eager, begierig *be-geer'-eeç*

ear, Ohr (n) *ohr*

earache, Ohrenschmerzen (m, pl) *ohr'-en-shmerts-en*

early, früh *frēū* [23]

earn v., verdienen *fer-deen'-en*

earrings, Ohrringe (m, pl) *ohr'-reeng-e*

earth, Erde (f) *ehr'-de*

easily, leicht *liçt*

east, Osten (m) *ost'-en*

Easter, Ostern (f, pl) *ost'-ern*

easy, leicht *liçt*

eat, essen *es'-en* [37, 48 51, 88]

edge, Schneide (f), Rand (m) *shnid'-e, rahnt*

egg, Ei (n) *i*

eight, acht *ahkht*

eighteen, achtzehn *ahkht'-tsehn*

eighth, achte *ahkht'-e*

eighty, achtzig *ahkht'-tseeç*

either, entweder *ent'-vehd-er* **either . . . or,** entweder
. . . oder *ent'-vehd-er . . . oh'-der*

elbow, Ellbogen (m) *el'-bohg-en*

electric, elektrisch *eh-lek'-treesh*

elevator, Aufzug (m), Fahrstuhl (m) *owf'-tsook fahr'-
shtool* [38]

eleven, elf *elf*

else: nobody else, niemand anders *nee'-mahnt ahnd'-ers*
nothing else, nichts anders *niçts ahnd'-ers* **something
else,** etwas anders *et'-vahs ahnd'-ers*

elsewhere, anderswo *ahnd'-ers-voh*

embark, einschiffen *in'-shif-en*

embarrassed, verlegen *fer-lehg'-en*

embassy, Botschaft (f) *boht'-shahft*

embrace *v.,* umarmen *um-ahrm'-en*

emergency, Notfall (m) *noht'-fahl*

empty, leer *lehr*

end *n.,* Ende (n), Schluss (m) *end'-e, shlus*

engaged [busy], beschäftigt *be-sheft'-eeçt;* [to be married],
verlobt *fer-lohpt'*

engine, Motor (m) *moh-tohr'*

English, englisch *ehng'-leesh*

enjoy, geniessen *ge-nees'-en*

enormous, enorm, ungeheuer *eh-nohrm', un'-ge-hoy-er*

enough, genug *ge-nookh'* **that's enough,** das genügt *dahs ge-néůkht'*

enter, hineingehen *hin-in'-geh-en*

entertaining, unterhaltend *un-ter-hahlt'-ent*

entire, ganz *gahnts*

entrance, Eingang (m), Einfahrt (f) *in'-gahng, in'-fahrt*

envelope, Briefumschlag (m) *breef'-um-shlahk*

equal, gleich *gliç*

equipment, Ausrüstung (f) *ows'-rêůst-oong*

error, Irrtum (m) *eer'-toom*

Europe, Europa *oy-roh'-pah*

even *adv.,* sogar, eben *zoh-gahr', ehb'-en*

even [number], gerade *ge-rah'-de*

evening, Abend (m) *ah'-bent* [99] **good evening,** guten Abend *goot'-en ah'-bent*

ever, je *yeh*

every, jeder *yehd'-er*

everyone, alle, jedermann *ahl'-e, yehd'-er-mahn*

everything, alles *ahl'-es*

everywhere, überall *êů-ber-ahl'*

evidently, offenbar, augenscheinlich *of'-en-bahr, owg'-en-shin-leeç*

exact, genau *ge-now'*

examination, Prüfung (f) *prêůf'-oong*

examine, prüfen *prêůf'-en*

example, Beispiel (n) *bi'-shpeel* **for example,** zum Beispiel *tsum bi'-shpeel*

excellent, ausgezeichnet *ows'-ge-tsiç-net*

except, ausgenommen, ausser *ows'-ge-nom-en, ows'-er*

exchange *v.,* austauschen *ows'-towsh-en*

exchange rate, Kurs (m) *kurs* [30]

excursion, Ausflug (m) *ows'-flook*

excuse *v.,* verzeihen *fer-tsi'-en* **excuse me,** verzeihung *fer-tsi'-oong*

exercise, Übung (f), Leibesübung (f) *êůb'-oong, lib'-es-êůb'-oong*

exhibition, Ausstellung (f) *ows'-shtel-oong* [98]
exit, Ausgang (m), Ausfahrt (f) *ows'-gahng, ows'-fahrt*
expect, erwarten *ehr-vahrt'-en* [31]
expensive, teuer *toy'-er* [37, 66, 73]
explain, erklären *ehr-klehr'-en*
explanation, Erklärung (f) *ehr-klehr-oong*
export *v.,* ausführen *ows'-fêur-en*
express [train], Schnellzug (m) *shnel'-tsook* [86]
extra, extra *eks'-trah*
extraordinary, ausserordentlich *ows-er-ohr'-dent-leeç*
eye, Auge (n) *ow'-ge*

face, Gesicht (n) *ge-ziçt'*
factory, Fabrik (f) *fah-breek'*
faint *v.,* in Ohnmacht fallen *in ohn'-mahkht fahl'-en*
fair [market], Messe (f) *mes'-e*
fall [season], Herbst (m) *herpst*
fall *v.,* fallen *fahl'-en*
false, falsch *fahlsh*
family, Familie (f) *fah-meel'-ye*
famous, berümt *be-rêumt'*
fan, Fächer (m) *feç'-er*
far, weit *vit* **so far,** so weit, bis jetzt *zoh vit, bis yetst* **how far is it?,** wie weit ist es? *vee vit ist es?*
fare [cost], Fahrpreis (m), Fahrgeld (n) *fahr'-pris, fahr'-gelt* [45]
farewell, Abschied (m) *ahp'-sheet*
farm, Bauernhof (m) *bow'-ern-hohf*
farmer, Bauer (m) *bow'-er*
farther, weiter *vit'-er*
fashion, Mode (f) *moh'-de*
fast [quick], schnell *shnel* [75]
fasten, befestigen *be-fest'-ee-gen*
fat, dick *dik*
father, Vater (m) *faht'-er* [2]
father-in-law, Schwiegervater (m) *shveeg'-er-faht-er*

fault, Schuld (f) *shult*
favor, Gunst (f), Gefallen (m) *gunst, ge-fahl'-en*
favorite *adj. & n.,* Lieblings- *leep'-leengs*
fear: to be afraid, sich fürchten *ziç fêûrçt'-en*
feather, Feder (f) *fehd'-er*
February, Februar (m) *feb'-roo-ahr*
fee, Gebühr (f) *ge-bêûr'*
feel, fühlen *fêûl'-en* [92]
feeling, Gefühl (n) *ge-fêûl'*
female, Weibchen (n) *vip'-çen*
feminine, weiblich *vip'-leeç*
fence, Zuan (m) *tsown*
fender, Kotflügel (m) *koht'-flêûg-el*
ferry [boat], Fähre (f) *feh'-re*
fever, Fieber (n) *feeb'-er* [94]
few, wenige, einige *veh'-nee-ge, i'-nee-ge*
field, Feld (n) *felt*
fifteen, fünfzehn *fêûnf'-tsehn*
fifth, fünfte *fêûnft'-e*
fifty, fünfzig *fêûnf'-tseeç*
fight *n.,* Kampf (m) *kahmpf*
fight *v.,* kämpfen *kempf'-en*
fill *v.,* füllen *fêûl'-en* [38]
filling [for a tooth], Plombe (f) *plomb'-e*
film, Film (m) *film*
final, endgültig *ent-gêûlt'-eeç*
finally, endlich *ent'-leeç*
find, finden *find'-en*
fine *adj.,* fein, vornehm *fin, for'-nehm*
fine *n.,* Geldstrafe (f) *gelt'-shtrahf-e* [76]
finger, Finger (m) *feeng'-er* [94]
finish *v.,* vollenden, beendigen *fol-end'-en, be-end'-ee-gen*
fire, Feuer (n) *foy'-er* [14]
first, erste *ehrst'-e* **first class,** erste Klasse *ehrst'-e klahs'-e* [85, 88]
fish, Fisch (m) *fish* [55]

fish v., fischen, angeln *fish'-en, ahng'-eln*
fish·bone, Gräte (f) *greht'-e*
fit [seizure], Anfall (m) *ahn'-fahl*
fit v., passen *pahs'-en*
fitting [of a garment], Probe (f) *prohb'-e*
five, fünf *fēūnf*
fix v., reparieren, verbessern *reh-pah-reer'-en, fer-bes'-ern* [74, 76]
flag, Fahne (f) *fah'-ne*
flashbulb, Photobirne (f) *foh'-toh-beer-ne*
flat, flach *flahkh*
flat tire, Reifenpanne (f), Platte (f) *rif'-en-pahn-e, plaht'-e* [74, 76]
flavor, Geschmack (m) *ge-shmahk'*
flight, Flug (m) *flook* [89, 90]
flint, Feuerstein (m) *foy'-er-shtin*
flirt v., liebeln, schäkeln *leeb'-eln, shehk'eln*
flood, Überschwemmung (f) *ēū'-ber-shvem-oong*
floor, Fussboden (m) *foos'-bohd-en*; [storey], Stock (m) *shtok*
florist, Blumenhändler (m) *bloom'-en-hent-ler*
flower, Blume (f) *bloom'-e*
fluid, Flüssigkeit (f) *flēūs'-eeç-kit*
fly [insect], Fliege (f) *fleeg'-e*
fly v., fliegen *fleeg'-en* [90]
fog, Nebel (m) *nehb'-el* [5]
follow, folgen *folg'-en*
food, Essen (n), Speise (f), Nahrung (f) *es'-en, shpiz'-e, nahr'-oong*
foot, Fuss (m) *foos*
for, für *fēūr*
forbid, verbieten *fer-beet'-en*
forbidden, verboten *fer-boht'-en*
forehead, Stirn (f) *shteern*
foreign, fremd *fremt*
foreigner, Ausländer (m) *ows'-lend-er*

forest, Wald (m), Forst (m) *vahlt, forst*
forget, vergessen *fer-ges'-en*
forgive, vergeben *fer-gehb'-en*
fork, Gabel (f) *gahb'-el* [53]
form, Form (f), Gestalt (f) *form, ge-shtahlt'*
former, ehemalig *eh'-e-mahl-eeç*
formerly, früher, ehemals *frêu'-er, eh'-e-mahlss*
fort, Festung (f) *fest'-oong*
fortunate, glücklich *glêuk'-leeç*
fortunately, glücklicherweise *glêuk'-leeç-er-viz-e*
forty, vierzig *feer'-tseeç*
forward, vorwärts *for'-verts*
fountain, Springbrunnen (m) *shpreeng'-brun-en*
four, vier *feer*
fourteen, vierzehn *feer'-tsehn*
fourth, vierte *feert'-e*
fracture *n.,* Bruch (m) *brookh*
fragile, zerbrechlich *tser-breç'-leeç*
free, frei *fri* [43]
freedom, Freiheit (f) *fri'-hit*
freeze, frieren, gefrieren *freer'-en, ge-freer'-en*
frequently, häufig *hoy'-feeç* [95]
fresh, frisch *frish* [51]
Friday, Freitag (m) *fri'-tahkh*
fried, gebraten *ge-braht'-en*
friend, Freund (m), Freundin (f) *froynt, froynd'-in* [2]
friendly, freundlich *froynt'-leeç*
from, von *fon*
front: in front of, vor *for*
frozen, gefroren *ge-frohr'-en*
fruit, Frucht (f), Obst (n) *frookht, ohpst* [51]
full, voll *fol*
fun, Spass (m) *shpahs*
function *v.,* funkzionieren *funk-tsee-oh-neer'-en*
funnel, Trichter (m) *triçt'-er*
funny, komisch *koh'-meesh*

fur, Pelz (m) *pelts*
furnished, möbliert *mōē-bleert'*
furniture, Möbel (f) *mōeb'-el*
further, ferner *fern'-er*
future, Zukunft (f) *tsoo'-kunft*

gain *v.,* gewinnen *ge-vin'-en*
gamble *v.,* spielen *shpeel'-en*
game, Spiel (n) *shpeel*
gangplank, Landungssteg (m), Laufplanke (f) *lahnd'-oongs-shtehk, lowf'-plahnk-e* [89]
garage, Garage (f) *gah-rah'-she* [73]
garden, Garten (m) *gahrt'-en*
garlic, Knoblauch (m) *knohp'-lowkh*
gas, Gas (n) *gahs*
gasoline, Benzin (n) *ben-tseen'* [73]
gas station, Tankstelle (f) *tahnk'-shtel-e* [73]
gate, Tor (n) *tohr*
gather [collect], sammeln *zahm'-eln*
gay, lustig *lust'-eeç*
general *adj.,* allgemein *ahl'-ge-min*
generally, in general, im allgemeinen, gewöhnlich *im ahl'-ge-min-en, ge-vōēn'-leeç*
generous, grossmütig, freigebig *grohs'-mēūt-eeç, fri'-gehb-eeç*
gentleman, Herr (m) *her*
get, kriegen, bekommen *kreeg'-en, be-kom'-en* **get in,** einsteigen *in'-shtig-en* **get off,** aussteigen *ows'-shtig-en* [44, 45] **get on,** einsteigen *in'-shtig-en* [45, 95] **get up,** aufstehen *owf'-shteh-en* [24, 95]
gift, Geschenk (n) *ge-shehnk'*
gin, Gin (m), Wacholderbranntwein (m) *jin, vahkh'-older-brahnt-vin*
girl, Mädchen (n) *meht'-çen* [9]
give, geben *gehb'-en* [11] **give me,** geben Sie mir *gehb'-en zee meer*

glad, froh *froh*

gladly, gerne, gern *gern'-e, gern*

glass [for drinking], Glas (n) *glahs* [50, 51, 54, 55]

glasses [for the eyes], Brille (f) *bril'-e*

glove, Handschuh (m) *hahnt'-shoo*

go, gehen *geh'-en* [11, 34, 101] **go back,** zurückkehren *tsoo-reûk'-kehr-en* **go in,** eintreten *in'-treht-en* [99] **go out,** ausgehen *ows'-geh-en*

God, Gott (m) *got*

gold, Gold (n) *golt*

good, gut *goot*

goodbye, auf Wiedersehen!, leben Sie wohl! *owf veed'-er-zeh-en, lehb'-en zee vohl*

government, Regierung (f) *reh-geer'-oong*

grandfather, Grossvater (m) *grohs'-faht-er*

grandmother, Grossmutter (f) *grohs'-mut-er*

grapes, Weintrauben (f, pl) *vīn'-trowb-en*

grapefruit, Pompelmuse (f) *pom-pel-mooz'-e*

grass, Gras (n) *grahs*

grateful, dankbar *dahnk'-bahr*

gray, grau *grow*

grease *n.,* Fett (n) *fet*

great, gross *grohs*

green, grün *grеûn*

grocery [store], Lebensmittelgeschäft (n) *lehb'-ens-mit-el-ge-sheft*

ground, Boden (m) *bohd'-en*

group, Gruppe (f) *grup'-e*

grow, wachsen *vahks'-en*

guard *v.,* bewachen *be-vahkh'-en*

guest, Gast (m) *gahst*

guide *n.,* Führer (m) *feûr'-er*

guilty, schuldig *shuld'-eeç*

guitar, Gitarre (f) *gee-tahr'-e*

gum [chewing], Kaugummi (f) *kow'-gu-mee*

gun, Gewehr (n) *ge-vehr'*

habit, Gewohnheit (f) *ge-vohn'-hĭt*
hair, Haar (n), Haare (n, pl) *hahr, hahr'-e*
haircut, Haarschneiden (n) *hahr'-shnĭd-en*
hairdresser, Friseur (m) *free-zōȇr'*
hairpin, Haarnadel (f) *hahr'-nahd-el*
half *adj.,* halb *hahlp*
half *n.,* Hälfte (f) *helft'-e*
hall, Gang (m) *gahng*
ham, Schinken (m) *sheenk'-en*
hand, Hand (f) *hahnt*
handkerchief, Taschentuch (n) *tahsh'-en-tookh* [39]
hand-made, angefertigt *ahn'-ge-fert-eeçt*
handsome, schön, stattlich *shöȇn, shtaht'-leeç* [9]
hang, hängen *hehng'-en* **hang up,** aufhängen *owf'-hehng-en*
hanger [for clothing], Kleiderbügel (m) *klĭd'-er-bȇug-el*
happen, geschehen *ge-sheh'-en* [14]
happy, glücklich, fröhlich, freudig *glȇuk'-leeç, frȏȇ'-leeç, froyd'-eeç*
harbor, Hafen (m) *hahf'-en* [87]
hard, hart *hahrt*
hardly, kaum *kown*
harm *n.,* Schaden (m) *shahd'-en*
harm *v.,* schaden *shahd'-en*
harmful, schädlich *shehd'-leeç*
haste, Eile (f) *i'-le*
hat, Hut (m) *hoot*
hat shop, Hutgeschäft (n) *hoot'-ge-sheft*
hate *v.,* hassen *hahs'-en*
have, haben *hahb'-en* **I have,** ich habe *iç hahb'-e* **have you?** haben Sie? *hahb'-en zee?*
he, er *ehr*
head, Kopf (m) *kopf*
headache, Kopfschmerzen (m, pl) *kopf'-shmerts-en* [92]
health, Gesundheit (f) *ge-zunt'-hĭt*
hear, hören *hōȇr'-en*

heart, Herz (n) *herts*

heat *n.,* Hitze (f) *hits'-e*

heavy, schwer *shvehr*

heel [of foot], Ferse (f) *fer'-ze*; [of shoe], Absatz (m) *ahp'-zahts*

hello, guten Tag *goot'-en tahkh*

help *n.,* Hilfe (f) *hilf'-e*

help *v.,* helfen *helf'-en* [13]

helpful, behilflich *be-hilf'-leeç*

hem *n.,* Saum (m) *zowm*

hen, Henne (f) *hen'-e*

her *adj.,* ihr *eer*

her *pron.,* sie *zee* **to her,** ihr *eer*

here, hier *heer*

hers, der (die, das) Ihre *dehr (dee, dahs) eer'-e*

high, hoch *hohkh*

hill, Hügel (m) *heüg'-el*

him, ihn *een* **to him,** ihm *eem*

hip, Hüfte (f) *heüft'-e*

hire, mieten *meet'-en* [72]

his, sein, der Seine *zin, dehr zin'-e*

history, Geschichte (f) *ge-shiçt'-e*

hit *v.,* schlagen *shlahg'-en*

hold, halten *hahlt'-en*

hole, Loch (n) *lokh*

holiday, Feiertag (m) *fi'-er-tahkh*

holy, heilig *hi'-leeç*

home, Heim (n) *him*; [at home], zu Hause, daheim *tsoo how'-ze, dah-him*

honest, ehrlich *ehr'-leeç*

honey [food], Honig (m) *hohn'-eeç*

honor, Ehre (f) *ehr'-e*

hope *n.,* Hoffnung (f) *hof'-noong*

hope *v.,* hoffen *hof'-en* [3]

horn [automobile], Hupe (f) *hoop'-e*

hors d'oeuvres, Vorspeisen (f, pl) *for'-shpiz-en*

horse, Pferd (n) *pfert*

hospital, Krankenhaus (n) *krahnk'-en-hows* [93]

host, Gastgeber (m) *gahst'-gehb-er*

hot, heiss *hiss* [6]

hotel, Hotel (n) *hoh-tel'* [9, 31, 35, 37, 44, 52, 69, 101]

hour, Stunde (f) *shtund'-e*

house, Haus (n) *hows*

how, wie *vee* **how are you?** wie geht es Ihnen? *vee geht es ee'-nen?* **how far?** wie weit? *vee vit?* **how long?** wie lange? *vee lahng'-e* **how many?** wieviele? *vee-feel'-e?* **how much?** wieviel? *vee-feel'?*

hug n., Umarmung (f) *um-ahrm'-oong*

human, menschlich *mehnsh'-leeç*

humid, feucht *foyçt*

hundred, hundert *hund'-ert*

hunger, Hunger (m) *hung'-er*

hungry, hungrig *hung'-reeç* [47, 48]

hurry: be in a hurry, Eile haben, es eilig haben *i'-le hahb'-en, es i'-leeç hahb'-en* **hurry up!** beeilen Sie sich!*b e-i'-len zee ziç*

hurt, weh tun, schmerzen *veh toon, shmerts'-en* [93, 94]

husband, Gatte (m), Mann (m) *gaht'-e, mahn* [2]

I, ich *iç*

ice, Eis (n) *is* [7, 55]

ice cream, Eis (n), Rahmeis (n) *is, rahm'-is* [55]

idea, Idee (f), Ahnung (f) *ee-deh', ah'-noong*

identification, Ausweis (m) *ows'-vis*

if, wenn *ven*

ill, krank *krahnk*

illegal, ungesetzlich, gesetzwidrig *un'-ge-zets-leeç, ge-zets'-veed-reeç*

illness, Krankheit (f) *krahnk'-hit*

imagine, sich vorstellen *ziç for'-shtel-en*

immediately, sofort, gleich *zoh-fort', gliç*

important, wichtig *viç'-teeç*

impossible, unmöglich *un-mŏĕg'-leeç* [12]
improve, verbessern *fer-bes'-ern*
improvement, Verbesserung (f) *fer-bes'-er-oong*
in, in *in*
incident, Vorfall (m) *for'-fahl*
included, inbegriffen, mitberechnet, einberechnet *in'-be-grif-en, mit'-be-reç-net, in'-be'-reç'-net* [37, 56]
incomplete, unvollständig *un'-fol'-shtend-eeç*
inconvenient, unbequem *un'-be-kvehm*
incorrect, unrichtig *un'-riçt-eeç*
increase *v.*, erhöhen, vermehren *ehr-hŏĕ'-en, fer-mehr'-en*
incredible, unglaublich *un-glowp'-leeç*
indeed, tatsächlich *taht-zeç'-leeç*
independence, Unabhängigkeit (f) *un-ahp-hehng'-eeç-kit*
independent, unabhängig *un'-ahp-hehng-eeç*
indicate, anzeigen *ahn'-tsig-en*
indigestion, Verdauungsstörung (f) *fer-dow'-oongs-shtŏĕr-oong*
indoors, drinnen *drin'-en*
industrial, industriell *in-doos-tree-el'*
inexpensive, wohlfeil *vohl'-fil*
infection, Ansteckung (f) *ahn'-shtek-oong*
infectious, ansteckend *ahn'-shtek-ent*
inform, benachrichtigen *be-nahkh'-riç-tee-gen*
information, Auskunft (f) *ows'-kunft*
injection, Einspritzung (f) *in'-shpritz-oong*
injury, Verletzung (f) *fer-lets'-oong*
injustice, Ungerechtigkeit (f) *un-ge-reç'-teeç-kit*
ink, Tinte (f) *tint'-e*
inn, Gasthof (m) *gahst'-hohf*
inquire, sich erkundigen *ziç ehr-kund'-ee-gen*
inside, drinnen, innerhalb *drin'-en, in'-er-hahlp*
insist, bestehen auf *be-shteh'-en owf*
inspect, beaufsichtigen *be-owf'-ziçt-ee-gen*
instead of, anstatt *ahn'-shtaht*
institution, Anstalt (f) *ahn'-shtahlt*

insurance, Versicherung (f) *fer-ziç'-er-oong* [73]
insure, versichern *fer-ziç'-ern*
intelligent, intelligent *in-tel-ee-gent'*
intend, beabsichtigen *be-ahp'-ziç-tee-gen*
intense, heftig, angespannt *heft'-eeç, ahn'-ge-shpahnt*
intention, Absicht (f) *ahp'-ziçt*
interest *n.,* Interesse (n) *in-te-res'-e*
interest *v.,* interessieren *in-te-res-ee'-ren*
interesting, interessant *in-te-res-ahnt'* [101]
intermission, Pause (f) *powz'-e*
internal, inner, innerlich *in'-er, in'-er-leeç*
international, international *in-ter-nah-tsee-oh-nahl'*
interpret, übersetzen *eū'-ber-zets-en*
interpreter, Dolmetscher (m) *dol'-metch-er*
interview *n.,* Unterredung (f) *un'-ter-rehd-oong*
into, in *in*
introduce, vorstellen *for'-shtel-en*
introduction, Vorstellung (f) *for'-shtel-oong*
investigate, untersuchen *un-ter-zookh'-en*
invitation, Einladung (f) *in'-lahd-oong*
invite, einladen *in'-lahd-en*
iron [for ironing], Bügeleisen (n) *beūg'-el-iz-en*
iron [metal], Eisen (n) *iz'-en*
iron *v.,* bügeln *beūg'-eln*
is: he is, er ist *ehr ist* **she is,** sie ist *zee ist* **it is,** es ist
island, Insel (f) *in'-zel*
it, es *es*
itch *v.,* jucken *yuk'-en*

jacket, Jacke (f) *yahk'-e* [6]
jail, Gefängnis (n) *ge-fehng'-nis*
jam, Marmelade (f) *mahr-me-lah'-de*
January, Januar (m) *yah'-noo ahr*
jaw, Kiefer (m) *keef'-er*
jelly, Gelee (n) *zhe-leh'*

jewelry, Schmuck (m), Schmucksachen (f, pl) *shmuk, shmuk'-zahkh-en*

jewelry store, Juwelenhandlung (f) *yoo-veh'-len-hahnt-loong*

job, Arbeit (f) *ahr'-bit*

joke, Witz (m), Scherz (m) *vits, sherts*

juice, Saft (m) *zahft*

July, Juli (m) *yoo'-lee*

jump *v.,* springen *shpreeng'-en*

June, Juni (m) *yoo'-nee*

just, gerecht *ge-reçt'*

justice, Gerechtigkeit (f) *ge-reçt'-eeç-kit*

keep, behalten *be-hahlt'-en*

key, Schlüssel (m) *shlêûs'-el* [33, 38, 73, 88]

kidneys, Nieren (f, pl) *neer'-en*

kill, töten *tôêt'-en*

kilogram, Kilogramm (n) *kee-loh-grahm'*

kilometer, Kilometer (n) *kee-loh-meht'-er* [72]

kind *adj.,* gütig, liebenswürdig *gêût'-eeç, leeb'-ens-veûrd-eeç*

kind *n.,* Art (f) *ahrt* [30]

king, König (m) *kôên'-eeç*

kiss *n.,* Kuss (m) *kus*

kiss *v.,* küssen *kêûs'-en*

kitchen, Küche (f) *kêûç'-e*

knee, Knie (n) *knee*

knife, Messer (n) *mes'-er* [53]

knock *v.,* klopfen *klopf'-en*

know [something], wissen *vis'-en* [89]; [someone], kennen *ken'-en* [89]

laborer, Arbeiter (m) *ahr'-bit-er*

lace Spitze (f) *shpits'-e*

ladies' room, Damentoilette (f) *dahm'-en-toy-let-e*

lady, Dame (f) *dahm'-e*

lake, See (m) *zeh*

lamb, Lamm (n) *lahm*

lame, lahm *lahm*

land *n.*, Land (n) *lahnt*

land *v.*, landen *lahnd'-en* [90]

landing card, Landungskarte (f) *lahnd'-oongs-kahrt-e* [89]

language, Sprache (f) *shprahkh'-e*

large, gross *grohs* [36]

last *adj.*, letzt *letst* [46]

last *v.*, dauern *dow'-ern* [98]

late, spät *shpeht* [23, 85, 96]

laugh *v.*, lachen *lahkh'-en*

laugh *n.*, Gelächter (n) *ge-leçt'-er*

laundry, Wäsche (f) *vesh'-e*

lavatory, Toilette (f), Klosett (n), Abort (m) *toy-let'-e,*
kloh-zet', ahp'-ort [86]

law, Gesetz (n) *ge-zets'*

lawyer, Rechtsanwalt (m) *reçts'-ahn-vahlt*

lazy, faul *fowl*

lead *v.*, führen *feür'-en* [99]

leaf, Blatt (n) *blaht*

leak *n.*, Leck (n) *lek*

learn, lernen *lern'-en*

least, wenigste *veh'-neek-ste*

leather, Leder (n) *lehd'-er*

leave, abreisen, lassen *ahp'-riz-en, lahs'-en* [39, 46, 73, 76,
84, 86, 89]

left, link *link* [45]

leg, Bein (n) *bin* [94]

lemon, Zitrone (f) *tsee-troh'-ne*

lend, leihen *li'-en*

length, Länge (f) *lehng'-e*

lens, Linse (f) *linz'-e*

less, weniger *veh'-neeg-er*

let, lassen *lahs'-en*

letter, Brief (m) *breef* [39]

lettuce, Kopfsalat (m), Lattich (m) *kopf'-zah-laht, laht'-eeç*

liberty, Freiheit (f) *fri'-hit*

library, Bibliothek (f) *beeb-lee-oh-tek'*

license, Bescheinigung (f), Führerschein (m) *be-shi'-nee-goong, feûr'-er-shin* [76]

lie: to lie down, sich hinlegen *ziç hin'-lehg-en* [95]

lie [untruth], Lüge (f) *leûg'-e*

lie *v.,* lügen *leûg'-en*

life, Leben (n) *lehb'-en*

lift *v.,* aufheben *owf'-hehb-en*

light [weight], leicht *liçt;* [color], hell *hel*

light *n.,* Licht (n), Scheinwerfer (m) *lict, shin'-verf-er*

lighter [cigarette], Feuerzeug (n) *foy'-er-tsoyk*

lightning, Blitz (m) *blits* [6]

like *adv.,* wie, ähnlich *vee, ehn'-leeç*

like *v.,* gern haben, gefallen *gern hahb'-en, ge-fahl'-en* [35, 66, 67, 101] **I would like,** ich möchte *iç môeç'-te*

line, Linie (f), Zeile (f) *leen'-ye, tsi'-le*

linen, Leinen (n) *lin'-en*

lip, Lippe (f) *lip'-e*

lipstick, Lippenstift (m) *lip'-en-shtift*

liquor, Schnaps (m) *shnahps*

list, Liste (f) *list'-e*

listen, zuhören, horchen *tsoo'-hoêr-en, hor'-çen*

little, klein *klin* **a little,** ein wenig, ein bisschen *in veh'-neeç, in bis'-çen* [10]

live *v.,* leben, wohnen *lehb'-en, wohn'-en* [9, 100]

liver, Leber (f) *lehb'-er*

lobby, Vorhalle (f) *for'-hahl-e*

lobster, Hummer (m) *hum'-er*

long, lang *lahng* [12, 37, 66, 68, 74, 76, 85, 94, 98]

look *v.,* schauen, sich ansehen *show'-en, ziç ahn'-zeh-en*

loose, lose, weit *lohz'-e, vit* [68]

lose, verlieren *fer-leer'-en*

lost, verloren *fer-lohr'-en* [14, 15, 38]
lot: a lot of, viel *feel*
lotion, Hautwasser (n) *howt'-vahs-er*
loud, laut *lowt*
love *n.,* Liebe (f) *leeb'-e*
love *v.,* lieben *leeb'-en* [9]
low, niedrig *need'-reeç*
lubricate *v.,* schmieren *shmeer'-en*
luck, Glück (n) *gleūk*　**good luck,** viel Glück *feel gleūk*
lucky, glücklich *gleūk'-leeç*　**to be lucky,** glücklich sein *gleūk'-leeç zin*
luggage, Gepäck (n) *ge-pek'* [34, 39, 43, 84]
lunch, Mittagessen (n) *mit'-tahk-es-en* [48]
lung, Lunge (f) *lung'-e*

machine, Maschine (f) *mah-sheen'-e*
madam, gnädige Frau *gneh'-dee-ge frow*
magazine, Zeitschrift (f) *tsīt'-shrift*
mail *n.,* Post (f) *post* [31]
mailbox, Briefkasten (m) *breef'-kahst-en*
main, haupt *howpt* **main course,** Hauptgericht (n) *howpt'-ge-riçt*
major, Major (m) *mah-yohr'*
make, machen *mahkh'-en* [41]
male, Männchen (n), männlich *men'-çen, men'-leeç*
man, Mensch (m), Mann (m) *mehnsh, mahn* [9, 14]
manager, Leiter (m), Geschäftsführer (m) *lit'-er, ge-shefts'-feūr-er*
manicure, Maniküre (f) *mah-nee-keūr'-e*
manner, Art (f), Weise (f) *ahrt, vīz'-e*
manufactured, hergestellt *hehr'-ge-shtelt*
many, viele *feel'-e*
map, Landkarte (f), Autokarte (f) *lahnt'-kahrt-e, ow'-toh-kahrt-e* [75]
marble, Marmor (m) *mahr'-mohr*
March, März (m) *merts*

mark *n.*, Marke (f), Zeichen (n) *mahrk'-e, tsïç'-en*
market, Markt (m) *mahrkt*
marketplace, Marktplatz (m) *mahrkt'-plahts*
marmalade, Marmelade (f) *mahr-me-lah'-de*
married, verheiratet *fer-hï-raht-et*
marry, heiraten *hï'-raht-en*
marvelous, wunderbar *vund'-er-bahr*
mass [church], Messe (f) *mes'-e*
message *n.*, Massage (f) *mah-sah'-zhe*
match, Streichholz (n), Zündholz (n) *shtrïç'-holts, tseûnt'-holts* [69]
material, Material (n) *mah-teh-ree-ahl'*
matter: no matter, keine Ursache *kïn'-e oor'-zahkh-e*
what is the matter? was ist los? *vahs ist lohs?*
May, Mai (m) *mï*
may, dürfen *deûrf'-en* **I may,** ich darf *iç dahrf* **may I?** darf ich? *dahrf iç?*
maybe, vielleicht *fee-lïçt'*
me, mich, mir *miç, meer* **to me,** zu mir *tsoo meer* **with me,** mit mir *mit meer*
meal, Mahlzeit (f) *mahl'-tsït* [37, 48, 52, 90]
mean *v.*, meinen, bedeuten *mïn'-en, be-doyt'-en* [12]
measure *n.*, Mass (n) *mahs*
measure *v.*, messen *mes'-en*
meat, Fleisch (n) *flïsh* [55]
mechanic, Mechaniker (m) *meh-khah'-neek-er* [74]
medicine, Arznei (f) *ahrts-nï'* [95]
medium, mittel, mittelschwer *mit'-el, mit'-el-shvehr*
meet, treffen, begegnen *tref'-en, be-gehg'-nen* [24]
melon, Melone (f) *me-loh'-ne*
member, Mitglied (n) *mit'-gleet*
memory, Gedächtnis (n) *ge-deçt'-nis*
mend, flicken, ausbessern *flik'-en, ows'-bes-ern*
men's room, Herrentoilette (f) *her'-en-toy-let-e*
mention *v.*, erwähnen *ehr-vehn'-en*
menu, Speisekarte (f) *shpïz'-e-kahrt-e* [50]

message, Mitteilung (f) *mit'-til-oong*
messenger, Bote (m) *boht'-e*
metal, Metall (n) *me-tahl'*
meter [measure], Meter (n) *meht'-er*
middle, Mitte (f) *mit'-e*
midnight, Mitternacht (f) *mit'-er-nahkht* [23]
mild, mild *milt*
milk, Milch (f) *milç* [51]
milliner, Modistin (f) *moh-dees'-tin*
million, Million (f) *meel-yohn'*
mind, Verstand (m), Sinn (m) *fer-shtahnt', zin*
mine, mein *min*
mineral, mineralisch *mee-ne-rah'-leesh*
mineral water, Mineralwasser (n) *mee-ne-rahl'-vahs-er*
minute, Minute (f) *mee-noot'-e*
mirror, Spiegel (m) *shpeeg'-el* [73]
misfortune, Unglück (n) *un'-gleŭk*
Miss, Fräulein (n) *froy'-lin*
missing, verfehlend *fer-fehl'-ent*
mistake *n.,* Fehler (m), Irrtum (m) *fehl'-er, eer'-tum* [56]
mistaken, irrtümlich, sich irren *eer'-teŭm-leeç, ziç eer'-en*
mix *v.,* mischen *mish'-en*
mixed, gemischt *ge-misht'*
model, Modell (n) *moh-del'*
modern, modern *moh-dern'*
modest, bescheiden *be-shid'-en*
moment, Augenblick (m) *ow'-gen-blik*
Monday, Montag (m) *mohn'-tahkh*
money, Geld (n) *gelt* [14, 31]
money order, Geldanweisung (f) *gelt'-ahn-viz-oong*
monk, Mönch (m) *mŏènkh*
month, Monat (m) *moh'-naht* **per month, a month,** pro Monat *proh moh'-naht*
monument, Denkmal (n) *dehnk'-mahl* [100]

moon, Mond (m) *mohnt* [7]

more, mehr *mehr*

morning, Morgen (m) *mor'-gen* [99, 101] **good morning,** guten Morgen *goot'-en mor'-gen*

most, am meisten, meist *ahn mīst'-en, mīst* **most of,** die meisten *dee mīst'-en*

mother, Mutter (f) *mut'-er* [2]

motion, Bewegung (f) *be-vehg'-oong*

motor, Motor (m) *moh-tohr'*

mountain, Berg (m) *berk*

mouth, Mund (m) *munt*

move *v.,* bewegen, sich bewegen, umziehen *be-vehg'-en, ziç be-vehg'-en, um'-tsee-en* [15]

movie, Kino (n) *kee'-noh* [100]

Mr., Herr (m) *her*

Mrs., Frau (f) *frow*

much, viel *feel* **too much,** zu viel *tsoo feel* **very much,** sehr viel *zehr feel* **how much?** wieviel? *vee-feel'*

mud, Schlamm (m) *shlahm*

muffler, Schalldämpfer (m) *shahl'-dempf-er*

muscle, Muskel (m) *mus'-kel*

museum, Museum (n) *moo-zeh'-oom* [46, 98]

mushroom, Pilz (m) *pilts*

music, Musik (f) *moo-zeek'*

musician, Musiker (m) *moo'-zeek-er*

must, müssen *mêûs'-en* **I must,** ich muss *iç mus*

mustache, Schnurrbart (m) *shnoor'-bahrt*

mustard, Senf (m), Mostrich (m) *zenf, mosh'-treeç*

mutton, Hammelfleisch (n) *hahm'-el-flish*

my, mein *min*

myself, mich, ich selbst *miç, iç zelpst*

nail [finger nail], Nagel (m) *nahg'-el*

nail file, Nagelfeile (f) *nahg'-el-fīl-e*

naked, nackt *nahkt*

name, Name (m) *nahm'-e* **last name,** Zuname (m) *tsoo'-nahm-e* **what is your name?** wie heissen Sie? *vee his'-en zee?* **my name is . . . ,** ich heisse . . . , *iç his'-e*

napkin, Serviette (f), Mundtuch (n) *ser-vee-et'-e, munt'-tookh* [54]

narrow, eng, schmal *ehng, shmahl* [68, 75]

nation, Nation (f) *nah-tsyon'*

national, national *nah-tsyon-ahl'*

nationality, Nationalität (f), Staatsangehörigkeit (f) *nah-tsyon-ah-lee-teht', shtahts'-ahn-ge-hö̂r-eeç-kit*

native, Eingeborene (m) *in'-ge-bohr-e-ne*

natural, natürlich *nah-teǔr'-leeç*

naturally, natürlich *nah-teǔr'-leeç*

nature, Natur (f) *nah-toor'*

near, nahe *nah'-e* [12, 29, 76, 93]

nearly, beinahe *bi-nah'-e*

necessary, notwendig, nötig *noht'-vend-eeç, nö̂et'-eeç*

neck, Hals (m) *hahlss*

necklace, Halsband (n) *hahlss'-bahnt*

necktie, Krawatte (f) *krah-vaht'-e*

need *v.,* brauchen, nötig sein *browkh'-en, nö̂et'-eeç zin* [91] **I need,** ich brauche, mir ist . . . nötig *iç browkh'-e, meer ist . . . nö̂et'-eeç*

needle, Nadel (f) *nahd'-el* [69]

neighbor, Nachbar (m) *nahkh'-bahr*

neighborhood, Nachbarschaft (f) *nahkh'-bahr-shahft*

neither . . . nor . . . , weder . . . noch *vehd'-er . . . nokh*

nephew, Neffe (m) *nef'-e*

nerve, Nerv (m) *nerf*

nervous, nervös *nerv-ö̂s'*

never, nie, niemals, nimmer *nee, nee'-mahls, nim'-er*

nevertheless, trotzdem, nichtsdestoweniger *trots'-dehm, niçts-des-toh-vehn'-eeg-er*

new, neu *noy*

news, Nachrichten (f, pl) *nahkh'-riçt-en*

newspaper, Zeitung (f) *tsit'-oong*

next *adj.,* nächster *neçst'-er*

next *adv.,* dann   *dahn*

nice, nett *net*

niece, Nichte (f) *niçt'-e*

night, Nacht (f) *nahkht*   **good night,** gute Nacht *goot'-e nahkht*

nightclub, Nachtlokal (n), Nachtklub (m) *nahkht'-loh-kahl, nahkht'-kloop*

nightgown, Nachthemd (n) *nahkht'-hemt*

nine, neun *noyn*

nineteen, neunzehn *noyn'-tsehn*

ninety, neunzig *noyn'-tseeç*

ninth, neunte *noynt'-e*

no, nein *nin*

noise, Lärm (m), Geräusch (n) *lehrm, ge-roysh'*

noisy, geräuschvoll *ge-roysh'-fol*

none, keiner, keine, keines *kin'-er, kin'-e, kin'-es*

noon, Mittag (m) *mit'-tahkh* [23]

no one, niemand *nee'-mahnt*

north, Norden (m) *nord'-en*

northeast, Nordosten (m) *nord-ohst'-en*

northwest, Nordwesten (m) *nord-vest'-en*

nose, Nase (f) *nahz'-e*

not, nicht *niçt*

notebook, Heft (n), Notizbuch (n) *heft, noh-teets'-bookh*

nothing, nichts *niçts*   **nothing else,** nichts anders, nichts weiteres *niçts ahnd'-ers, niçts vit'-er-es*

notice *n.,* Benachrichtigung (f), Ankündigung (f), Bekanntmachung (f) *be-nahkh'-riçt-ee-goong, ahn'-keünd-ee-goong, be-kahnt'-mahkh-oong*

notice *v.,* bemerken *be-merk'-en*

notify, benachrichtigen *be-nahkh'-riçt-ee-gen*

novel [book], Roman (m) *roh-mahn'*

November, November (m) *noh-vem'-ber*

novocaine, Novocain (n) *noh-voh-kah-een'*

now, jetzt, nun *yetst, noon* [48, 50, 98]
nowhere, nirgends *neer'-gents*
number, Nummer (f) *num'-er* [38, 41, 45]
nun, Nonne (f) *non'-e* [87, 89]
nurse, Krankenschwester (f) *krahnk'-en-shvest-er*
nursemaid, Kindermädchen (n) *kind'-er-meht-çen*
nut, nuts, Nuss, Nüsse (f) *nus, neûs'-e*

obey, gehorchen *ge-horç'-en*
obliged, verpflichtet *fer-pfliçt'-et*
obtain, erhalten, bekommen *ehr-hahlt'-en, be-kom'-en*
obvious, klar, offenbar *klahr, of'-en-bahr*
occasionally, gelegentlich, ab und zu *ge-lehg'-ent-leeç, ahp unt tsoo*
occupation, Beschäftigung (f), Beruf (m) *be-sheft'-ee-goong, be-roof'*
occupied, besetzt *be-zetst'* [85]
ocean, Ozean (m) *oh-tseh-ahn'* [36]
October, Oktober (m) *ok-toh'-ber*
odd [number], ungerade *un'-ge-rah-de*; [unusual], sonderbar *zond'-er-bahr*
of, von *fon*
offer *v.*, anbieten *ahn'-beet-en*
office, Büro (n) *beû-roh'*
official *adj.*, amtlich *ahmt'-leeç*
often, oft *oft* [5]
oil, Öl (n) *öel* [74]
old, alt *ahlt*
olive, Olive (f) *oh-leev'-e*
omelet, Omelette (f) *oh-me-let'-e*
on, auf *owf*
once, einmal *in'-mahl*
one, ein, eine, eins *in, in'-e, ins*
one way [street], Einbahnstrasse (f) *in'-bahn-shtras-e*; [ticket], einfache Fahrkarte (f) *in'-fahrk-e fahr'-kahr-te*
onion, Zwiebel (f) *tsveeb'-el*

only, nur *noor*

open *adj.,* offen, geöffnet *of'-en, ge-öēf'-net*

open *v.,* öffnen, aufmachen *öēf'-nen, owf'-mahkh-en* [33, 38, 61, 85, 98, 99]

opera, Oper (f) *oh'-per*

operation, Operation (f) *oh-pe-rah-tsyohn'*

operator [telephone], Telefonfräulein (n), Telefonistin (f) *teh-leh-fohn'-froy-lin, teh-leh-neest'-in*

opinion, Meinung (f) *mīn'-oong*

opportunity, Gelegenheit (f) *ge-lehg'-en'-hīt*

opposite, gegenüber, Gegenteil (n) *gehg-en-ēū'-ber, gehg'-en-til*

optician, Optiker (m) *op'-teek-er*

or, oder *oh'-der*

orange, Apfelsine (f) *ahpf-el-zeen'-e*

order *v.,* bestellen *be-shtel'-en* [55]

ordinary, gewöhnlich *ge-vöēn'-leeç*

oriental, orientalisch *oh-ree-en-tahl'-eesh*

original, ursprünglich *oor'-shprēūng-leeç*

ornament, Verzierung (f), Zierde (f) *fer-tseer'-oong, tseerd'-e*

other, anderer, andere *ahnd'-er-er, ahnd'-er-e*

ought, sollen *sohl'-en*

our, ours, unser, der Unsere *unz'-er, dehr unz'-er-e*

out *adv.,* aus, draussen *ows, drows'-en*

outdoor, im Freien *im frī'-en*

out of order, kaputt *kah-put'*

outside *adv.,* draussen *drows'-en* **outside of,** aus dem, aus der, aus den *ows dehm, ows dehr, ows dehn*

over [ended] *adj.,* vorbei, vollendet *for-bī', fol'-end-et*

over [above] *prep.,* über *ēū'-ber*

overcharge *n.,* überfordern, überteuern *ēū'-ber-ford-ern, ēū'-ber-toy-ern*

overcoat, Überzieher (m), Mantel (m) *ēū'-ber-tsee-er, mahnt'-el*

overcooked, zu viel durchgebraten *tsoo feel doorç'-ge-braht-en*

overturn, umstürzen *um'-shteurts-en*

owe, schulden *shuld'-en* [56]

own *adj.,* eigen *ig'-en*

owner, Eigentümer (m), Besitzer (m) *ig'-en-teūm-er, be-zits'-er*

oyster, Auster (f) *owst'-er*

pack *v.,* einpacken, packen *in'-pahk-en, pahk'-en* [69]

package, Paket (n) *pahk-eht'*

page, Seite (f) *zit'-e*

paid, bezahlt *be-tsahlt'*

pain, Schmerz (m) *shmerts*

paint, Farbe (f) *fahrb'-e*

paint *v.,* malen, anstreichen *mahl'-en, ahn'-shtrikh-en*

painting, Gemälde (n) *ge-meld'-e*

pair, Paar (n) *pahr* [68]

palace, Palast (m) *pah-lahst'* [100]

pale, blass *blahs*

pants, Hose (f) *hohz'-e*

paper, Papier (n) *pah-peer'*

parcel, Paket (n) *pahk-eht'*

pardon, Verzeihung (f) *fer-tsi-oong* **pardon me,** verzeihen Sie mir *fer-tsi'-en zee meer*

parents, Eltern (pl) *elt'-ern*

park *n.,* Park (m) *pahrk* [100]

park [a car] *v.,* parken *pahrk'-en* [76]

parsley, Petersilie (f) *peht-er-zeel'-ye*

part *n.,* Teil (m & n) *til*

particular, besonder *be-zond'-er*

partner [business], Teilhaber (m) *til'-hahb-er*

party, Partei (f), Fest (n) Abendgesellschaft (f) *pahr-ti', fest, ah'-bent-ge-zel-shahft*

pass *v.,* vorbeigehen, vorbeifahren *for-bi'-geh-en, for-bi'-fahr-en*

passage, Durchgang (m) *doorç'-gahng*

passenger, Passagier (m), Reisende (m) *pah-sah-zheer', riz'-end-e*

passport, Pass (m), Reisepass (m) *pahs, riz'-e-pahs* [15, 30, 32]

past *adj.,* vergangen *fer-gahng'-en*

past *n.,* Vergangenheit (f) *fer-gahng'-en-hit*

pastry, Gebäck (n) *ge-bek'*

path, Pfad (m) *pfaht*

patient *adj.,* geduldig *ge-duld'-eeç*

patient *n.,* Kranke (m, f) *krahnk'-e*

pay *v.,* zahlen, bezahlen *tsahl'-en, be-tsahl'-en* [33, 34, 56, 76] **to pay cash,** bar zahlen, bar bezahlen *bahr tsahl'-en, bahr be-tsahl'-en* [70]

payment, Zahlung (f) *tsahl'-oong*

pea, Erbse (f) *erp'-se*

peace, Frieden (m) *freed'-en*

peaceful, friedlich, ruhig *freet'-leeç, roo'-eeç*

peach, Pfirsich (m) *pfeer'-ziç*

peak, Gipfel (m) *gipf'-el*

peanut, Erdnuss (f) *erd'-nus*

pear, Birne (f) *beer'-ne*

pearl, Perle (f) *per'-le*

peculiar, sonderbar, seltsam *zond'-er-bahr, zelt'-zahm*

pen, Feder (f), Füllfeder (f) *fehd'-er, feül'-fehd-er* **fountain pen,** Füllfeder (f) *feül'-fehd-er*

penalty, Strafe (f) *shtrahf'-e*

pencil, Bleistift (m) *bli'-shtift*

penny, Pfennig (m) *pfen'-eeç*

people, Leute (pl), Volk (n) *loyt'-e, folk*

pepper, Pfeffer (m) *pfef'-er*

peppermint, Pfefferminz (n) *pfef'-er-mints*

per, pro *proh*

perfect, vollkommen *fol'-kom-en*

performance, Aufführung (f), Leistung (f) *owf'-feür-oong, list'-oong*

perfume, Parfüm (n) *pahr-feum'*
perfumery, Parfümerie (f) *pahr-feum-e-ree'*
perhaps, vielleicht *fee-liçt'*
period, Periode (f) *peh-ree-oh'-de*
permanent, ständig, dauernd *shtend'-eeç, dow'-ernt*
permission, Erlaubnis (m) *ehr-lowb'-nis*
permit *v.,* erlauben, gestatten *ehr-lowb'-en, ge-shtaht'-en*
person, Person (f) *per-zohn'*
personal, persönlich *per-zoen'-leeç* [33]
perspiration, Schweiss (m) *shvis*
petrol, Petroleum (n) *peh-troh'-leh-oom*
petticoat, Unterrock (m) *un'-ter-rok*
pharmacist, Apotheker (m) *ah-poh-tehk'-er*
pharmacy, Apotheke (f) *ah-poh-tehk'-e*
photograph, Photographie (f), Aufnahme (f) *foh-toh-grah-fee', owf'-nahm-e*
photographer, Photograph (m) *foh-toh-grahf'*
photography, Photographie (f) *foh-toh-grah-fee'*
photography shop, Photographieladen (m) *foh-toh-grah-fee'-lahd-en*
piano, Klavier (n) *klah-veer'*
pick [choose], wählen *vehl'-en*
pick up *v.,* aufheben, aufnehmen *owf'-hehb-en, owf'-nehm-en*
picture, Bild (n) *bilt*
pie, Torte (f) *tort'-e*
piece, Stück (n) *shteuk*
pier, Pier (m) *peer* [87]
pig, Schwein (n) *shvin*
pigeon, Taube (f) *towb'-e*
pile, Haufen (m) *howf'-en*
pill, Pille (f) *pil'-e*
pillar, Säule (f) *zoyl'-e*
pillow, Kopfkissen (n) *kopf'-kis-en* [90]
pilot, Pilot (m), Lotse (m) *pee-loht', loh'-tse*

pin, Stecknadel (f) *shtek'-nahd-el* [69] **safety pin,** Sicherheitsnadel (f) *ziç'-er-hits-nahd-el*

pineapple, Ananas (f) *ah'-nah-nahs*

pink, rosa *roh'-zah*

pipe [tobacco], Pfeife (f) *pfif'-e*

place *n.*, Platz (m), Ort (m) *plahts, ort* [98]

place *v.*, stellen, legen, setzen *shtel'-en, lehg'-en, zets'-en*

plain [simple], einfach *in'-fahkh*

plan *n.*, Plan (m) *plahn*

plant, Pflanze (f) *pflahnts'-e*

plastic, plastisch *plahs'-teesh*

plate, Teller (m) *tel'-er*

platform, Bahnsteig (m) *bahn'-shtik* [84]

play *v.*, spielen *shpeel'-en*

pleasant, angenehm *ahn'-ge-nehm*

please [suit or satisfy], gefallen *ge-fahl'-en* **if you please,** *bitte bit'-e*

pleasure, Vergnügen (n) *ferg-nêug'-en* [3]

plenty of, genug *ge-nookh'*

plum, Pflaume (f) *pflowm'-e*

pneumonia, Lungenentzündung (f) *lung'-en-ent-tsêund-oong*

poached, ohne Schale *oh'-ne shahl'-e*

pocket, Tasche (f) *tahsh'-e*

pocketbook, Handtasche (f) *hahnt'-tahsh-e*

point *n.*, Punkt (m), Spitze (f) *punkt, shpits'-e*

poison, Gift (n) *gift*

poisonous, giftig *gift'-eeç*

police, Polizei (f) *poh-lee-tsi'* [14]

policeman, Polizist (m), Schutzmann (m) *poh-lee-tsist', shuts'-mahn*

police station, Polizeiamt (n) *poh-lee-tsi'-ahmt*

political, politisch *poh-lee'-teesh*

pond, Teich (m) *tiç*

pool, Teich (m), Schwimmbad (n) *tiç, shvim'-baht* [88]

poor, arm *ahrm*

popular, volkstümlich, beliebt *folk'-shtēum-leeç, be-leept'*

pork, Schweinefleisch (n) *shvīn'-e-flish*

port, Hafen (m) *hahf'-en* [87]

porter, Gepäckträger (m) *ge-pek'-trehg-er* [34, 83, 84]

portrait, Bildnis (n) *bilt'-nis*

position, Stellung (f), Lage (f) *shtel'-oong, lahg'-e*

positive, bestimmt *be-shtimt'*

possible, möglich *mōēg'-leeç* [12]

possibly, möglicherweise *mōēg'-leeç-er-vīz-e*

postage, Porto (n) *por'-toh*

postage stamp, Briefmarke (f) *breef'-mahrk-e* [39]

postcard, Postkarte (f), Ansichtskarte (f) *post'-kahrt-e,*
   ahn'-ziçts-kahrt-e

post office, Postamt (n) *post'-ahmt*

potato, Kartoffel (f) *kahr-tof'-el*

pound [money], Pfund (n) *pfunt*

powder, Puder (m), Gesichtspuder (m) *pood'-er, ge-*
   ziçts'-pood-er

power, Macht (f) *mahkht*

powerful, mächtig *meçt'-eeç*

practical, praktisch *prahk'-teesh*

practice *v.*, üben *ēub'-en*

prayer, Gebet (n) *ge-beht'*

precious, kostbar, edel *kost'-bahr, ehd'-el*

prefer, vorziehen *for'-tsee-en*

preferable, vorzuziehend *for-tsoo'-tsee-ent*

pregnant, schwanger *shvahng'-er*

premier, Ministerpräsident (m) *mee-nees-tehr'-preh-zee-*
   dent

preparation, Vorbereitung (f) *for'-be-rīt-oong*

prepare, vorbereiten *for'-be-rīt-en*

prepay, vorauszahlen *for-ows'-tsahl-en*

prescription, Rezept (n) *reh-tsept'* [95]

present [gift], Geschenk (n) *ge-shehnk'*; [time], Gegenwart
   (f) *gehg'-en-vahrt*

present *v.*, vorstellen *for'-shtel-en* [2]
press [clothes], *v.*, bügeln *bûg'-eln*
pressure, Druck (m) *druk*
pretty, hübsch *hêupsh* [9]
prevent, verhindern, verhüten *fer-hind'-ern, fer-hêut'-en*
previous, früherer, vorhergehend *frêu'-er-er, for-hehr'-geh-ent*
price, Preis (m) *prīs* [36, 37]
priest, Priester (m), Pfarrer (m) *preest'-er, pfahr'-er*
principal, haupt *howpt*
prison, Gefängnis (n) *ge-fehng'-nis*
prisoner, Gefangene (m, f) *ge-fahng'-e-ne*
private, privat *pree-vaht'*
prize, Preis (m) *prīs*
probable, wahrscheinlich *vahr'-shīn-leeç*
probably, wahrscheinlich *vahr'-shīn-leeç*
problem, Problem (n) *proh-blehm'*
produce *v.*, vorbringen, herbringen *for'-breeng-en, her'-breeng-en*
production, Herstellung (f) *hehr'-shtel-oong*
profession, Beruf (m) *be-roof'*
professor, Professor (m) *proh-fes'-ohr*
program *n.*, Programm (n) *proh-grahm'*
progress *n.*, Fortschritt (m) *fort'-shrit*
promenade, Spaziergang (m) *shpah-tseer'-gahng*
promise *n.*, Versprechen (n) *fehr-shpreç'-en*
prompt, pünktlich *pêunkt'-leeç*
pronunciation, Aussprache (f) *ows'-shprahkh-e*
proof, Beweis (m) *be-vīs'*
proper, eigentümlich, *ī'-gen-têum-leeç*
property, Eigentum (n) *ī'-gen-toom*
proposal, Vorschlag (m) *for'-shlahk*
proprietor, Eigentümer (m), Inhaber (m) *ī'-gen-têum-er, in'-hahb-er*
prosperity, Wohlergehen (n) *vohl'-ehr-geh-en*
protect, schützen *shêuts'-en*

protection, Schutz (m) *shuts*
protestant *adj.*, protestantisch *proh-tes-tahn'-teesh*
proud, stolz *shtolts*
provide, nachweisen *nahkh'-vīz-en*
province, Gebiet (n) *ge-beet'*
provision, Beschaffung (f) *be-shahf'-oong*
prune, Backpflaume (f) *bahk'-pflow-me*
public, öffentlich *öef'-ent-leeç*
publish, veröffentlichen, herausgeben *fer-öef'-ent-leeç-en,*
  hehr-ows'-gehb-en
pull *v.*, ziehen *tsee'-en*
pump, Pumpe *pump'-e*
punish, bestrafen, strafen *be-shtrahf'-en, shtrahf'-en*
pupil, Schüler (m), Schülerin (f) *shéul'-er, shéul'-er-in*
purchase *n.*, Einkauf (m) *in'-kowf*
purchase *v.*, kaufen *kowf'-en*
pure, rein *rīn*
purple, purpurn *poor'-poorn*
purpose *n.*, Zweck (m), Absicht (f) *tsvek, ahp'-ziçt*
purse, Geldtasche (f), Geldbeutel (m) *gelt'-tahsh-e, gelt'-*
  boyt-el
purser, Zahlmeister (m) *tsahl'-mīst-er*
push *n.*, Stoss (m) *shtohs*
push *v.*, stossen *shtohs'-en*
put, legen, stellen, stecken *lehg'-en, shtel'-en, shtek'-en* [74]

quality, Qualität (f) *kvah-lee-teht'*
quantity, Quantität (f) *kvahn-tee-teht'*
quarrel *n.*, Streit (m) *shtrīt*
quarrel *v.*, streiten *shtrīt'-en*
quarter *adj. & n.*, Viertel (n) *feert'-el*
queen, Königin (f) *köen'-ee-gin*
question *n.*, Frage (f) *frahg'-e*
quick, schnell, rasch *shnel, rahsh*
quickly, schnell *shnel*

quiet, ruhig, still *roo'-eeç, shtil* [36]
quite, ganz *gahnts*

radio, Radio (n), Rundfunk (m) *rah'-dee-oh, runt'-funk*
railroad, Eisenbahn (f) *iz'-en-bahn*
railroad car, Eisenbahnwagen (m) *iz'-en-bahn-vahg-en*
railroad station, Bahnhof (m) *bahn'-hohf* [44, 83]
rain *n.,* Regen (m) *rehg'-en*
rain *v.,* regnen *rehg'-nen* [5, 101]
rainbow, Regenbogen (m) *rehg'-en-bohg-en* [7]
raincoat, Regenmantel (m) *rehg'-en-mahnt-el* [6]
raise *v.,* erhöhen, heben *ehr-hōē'-en, hehb'-en*
rapidly, schnell *shnel*
rare, selten *zelt'-en*
rash *n.,* Hautausschlag (m) *howt'-ows-shlahk*
raspberry, Himbeere (f) *him'-behr-e*
rate, Kurs (m) *kurs* [30]
rather, eher, lieber, ziemlich *eh'-er, leeb'-er, tseem'-leeç*
raw, roh *roh*
razor, Rasiermesser (n) *rah-zeer'-mes-er*
razor blade, Rasierklinge (f) *rah-zeer'-kleeng-e*
reach *v.,* erreichen, reichen *ehr-riç'-en, riç'-en*
read, lesen *lehz'-en*
ready, fertig, bereit *fert'-eeç, be-rit'* [48, 78]
real, wirklich *veerk'-leeç*
really, wirklich *veerk'-leeç*
rear, hinter *hin'-ter*
reason *n.,* Grund (m) *grunt*
reasonable, vernünftig *fer-nēunft'-eeç*
receipt, Quittung (f) *kvit'-oong* [31]
receive, empfangen, bekommen *emp-fahng'-en, be-kom'-en*
recent, neu *noy*
reception desk, Empfangsbüro (n) *emp-fahngs'-bēu-roh*
recognize, erkennen *ehr-ken'-en*

recommend, empfehlen *emp-fehl'-en* [50]

reconfirm [a flight], wieder bestätigen *veed'-er be-shteht'-ee-gen* [89]

recover, sich erholen *ziç ehr-hohl'-en*

red, rot *roht*

reduce, herabsetzen, verkleinern `hehr-ahp'-zets-en, fer-klin'-ern`

reduction, Nachlass (m), Herabsetzung (f) *nahkh'-lahs, hehr-ahp'-zets-oong*

refreshments, Erfrischungen *ehr-frish'-oong-en*

refund *v.,* zurückzahlen *tsoo-réûk'-tsahl-en*

refuse *v.,* ablehnen, verweigern *ahp-lehn'-en, fer-vig'-ern*

region, Gegend (f) *gehg'-ent*

register *n.,* Register (n) *reh-gees'-ter*

register [a letter], einschreiben *in'-shrib-en*; [at a hotel], sich einschreiben lassen *ziç in'-shrib-en lahs'-en*

regret, *v.,* bedauern *be-dow'-ern*

regular, regelmässig, gewöhnlich *rehg'-el-mes-eeç, ge-vȫen'-leeç*

regulation, Vorschrift (f) *for'-shrift*

relative [kin], Verwandte (m) *fer-vahnt'-e*

religion, Religion (f) *reh-lee-gee-ohn'*

remark *n.,* Bemerkung (f) *be-merk'-oong*

remember, sich erinnern *ziç ehr-in'-ern*

remove, entfernen, beseitigen *ent-fern'-en, be-zit'-ee-gen*

renew, erneuern *ehr-noy'-ern*

rent *v.,* mieten *meet'-en*

repair *v.,* reparieren, ausbessern *reh-pah-reer'-en, ows'-bes-ern*

repeat *v.,* wiederholen *veed'-er-hohl-en* [10]

replace [put back], wieder hinstellen, wieder einsetzen *veed'-er hin'-shtel-en, veed'-er in'-zets-en*

reply *n.,* Antwort (f) *ahnt'-vort*

republic, Republik (f) *reh-poob-leek'*

request *v.,* bitten, ersuchen *bit'-en, ehr-zookh'-en*

rescue *v.*, retten *ret'-en*

reservation, Vorbestellung (f), Vorbehalt (m) *for'-be-shtel-oong, for'-be-hahlt*

reserve *v.*, belegen, reservieren *be-lehg'-en, reh-zer-veer'-en* [53]

reserved, reserviert, belegt *reh-zer-veert', be-lehkht'*

residence, Wohnstätte (f) *vohn'-shtet-e*

resident, Bewohner (m) *be-vohn'-er*

responsible, verantwortlich *fer-ahnt'-vort-leeç*

rest *n.*, Ruhe (f) *roo'-e*

rest *v.*, sich ausruhen *ziç ows'-roo-en*

restaurant, Restaurant (n) *res-toh-rahng'* [37, 48]

restless, unruhig, ruhelos *un'-roo-iç, roo'-e-lohs*

rest room, Waschraum (m) *vahsh'-rowm*

result *n.*, Ergebnis (n) *ehr-gehp'-nis*

return *v.*, zurückkehren *tsoo-rêuk'-kehr-en* [44]

return ticket, Rückfahrkarte (f) *rêuk'-fahr-kahrt-e*

review *n.*, Überblick (m), Rundschau (f) *êu'-ber-blik, runt'-show*

reward, Belohnung (f) *be-lohn'-oong*

rib, Rippe (f) *rip'-e*

ribbon, Band (n) *bahnt*

rice, Reis (m) *ris*

rich, reich *riç*

ride *n.*, Fahrt (f) *fahrt* [44]

right [correct], richtig *riçt'-eeç* **to be right**, Recht haben *reçt hahb'-en* [12] **all right**, gut! *goot!* **to the right**, nach rechts *nahkh reçts*

right [direction], rechts *reçts* [45]

ring *n.*, Ring (m) *reeng*

ring *v.*, klingeln, läuten *kleeng'-eln, loyt'-en*

ripe, reif *rif*

rise *v.*, aufstehen *owf'-shteh-en*

river, Fluss (m) *flus* [100, 101]

road, Weg (m), Strasse (f) *vehkh, shtrahs'-e* [75]

roast [meat], braten *braht'-en*
rob, bestehlen, berauben *be-shtehl'-en, be-rowb'-en* [14]
robber, Räuber (m) *royb'-er*
rock, Felsen (m) *felz'-en*
roll [bread], Brötchen (n) *brȫet'-çen*
roll *v.,* rollen *rol'-en*
roof, Dach (n) *dahkh*
room, Zimmer (n) *tsim'-er* [35, 36, 38, 48]
rope, Seil (n), Strick (m) *zil, shtrik*
rose, Rose (f) *rohz'-e*
rouge, Schminke (f) *shmeenk'-e*
rough, stürmisch, rauh, grob *shteurm'-eesh, row, grohp*
round, rund *runt*
round trip, Hin- und Rückfahrt (f) *hin unt rēuk'-fahrt* [85]
royal, königlich *kȫen'-eek-leeç*
rubber, Gummi (m) *gum'-ee*
rude, grob *grohp*
rug, Teppich (m) *tep'-eeç*
ruin *v.,* zugrunde richten *tsoo'-grund-e riçt'-en*
rum, Rum (m) *room*
run *v.,* rennen, laufen *ren'-en, lowf'-en* [76]
runway, Rollbahn (f) *rol'-bahn* [90]

sad, traurig *trow'-reeç*
safe, sicher *ziç'-er*
safety pin, Sicherheitsnadel (f) *ziç'-er-hits-nahd-el*
sail *v.,* abreisen, segeln *ahp'-riz-en, zehg'-eln* [87]
sailor, Matrose (m) *mah-trohz'-e*
saint, Heilige (m) *hi'-lee-ge*
salad, Salat (m) *zah-laht'*
sale, Verkauf (m) *fer-kowf'* [67]   **for sale,** zu verkaufen
   tsoo fer-kowf'-en
sales girl, Verkäuferin (f) *fer-koyf'-er-in*
salesman, Verkäufer (m) *fer-koyf'-er*
salmon, Lachs (m) *lahks*
salt, Salz (n) *zahlts*

same, derselbe, dieselbe, dasselbe *dehr-zelb'-e, dee-zelb'-e, dahs-zelb'-e* **the same as,** dasselbe wie *dahs-zelb'-e vee*

sample *n.,* Muster (n) *must'-er*

sand, Sand (m) *zahnt*

sandwich, belegtes Brötchen (n) *be-lehkht'-es brōet'-çen*

sanitary, sanitär *zah-nee-tehr'*

sanitary napkin, Binde (f) *bind'-e*

satin, Seidensatin *zid-en-zah-teen'*

satisfactory, zufriedenstellend, befriedigend *tsoo-freed'-en-shtel-ent be-free'-dee-gent*

satisfied, befriedigt, zufrieden *be-free'-deeçt, tsoo-freed'-en*

satisfy, befriedigen *be-free'-dee-gen*

Saturday, Samstag (m) *zahms'-tahkh*

sauce, Sosse (f) *zohs'-e*

saucer, Untertasse (f) *un'-ter-tahs-e*

sausage, Wurst (f) *vurst*

save [money], sparen *shpahr'-en*; [rescue], retten *ret'-en*

say, sagen *zahg'-en* [10]

scale, Massstab (m), Waage (f) *mahs'-shtahp, vahg'-e*

scar *n.,* Narbe (f) *nahrb'-e*

scarce, knapp *knahp*

scarcely, kaum *kowm*

scare *v.,* erschrecken, scheuchen *ehr-shrek'-en, shoyç'-en*

scarf, Schal (m) *shahl*

scenery, Landschaft (f) *lahnt'-shahft*

scent *n.,* Geruch (m), Duft (m) *ge-rookh', duft*

schedule *n.,* Tabelle (f), Fahrplan (m) *tah-bel'-e, fahr'-plahn*

school, Schule (f) *shool'-e*

science, Wissenschaft (f) *vis'-en-shahft*

scientist, Wissenschaftler (m) *vis'-en-shahft-ler*

scissors, Schere (f) *shehr'-e*

scrape [injury], Kratzwunde (f) *krahts'-vund-e*

scratch *n.,* kratzen *krahts'-en*

sculpture, Bildhauerkunst (f) *bilt'-how-er-kunst*

sea, Meer (n), See (f) *mehr, zeh*

seafood, Fischgericht (n) *fish'-ge-riçt*

seagull, Möwe (f) *möev'-e*

seam, Naht (f) *haht*

seaport, Seehafen (m) *zeh'-hahf-en*

search *v.,* suchen *zookh'-en*

seasick, seekrank *zeh'-krahnk* [89]

season, Jahreszeit (f) *yahr'-es-tsit*

seat, Sitz (m), Sitzplatz (m) *zits, zits'-plahts* [85]

second, zweite *tsvit'-e* **second class,** zweite Klasse
tsvit'-e klahs'-e [85, 88]

secret *adj.,* geheim *ge-him'*

secret *n.,* Geheimnis (n) *ge-him'-nis*

secretary, Sekretär (m), Sekretärin (f) *zek-reh-tehr', zek-
reh-tehr'-in*

section, Abschnitt (m) *ahp'-shnit*

see, sehen *zeh'-en* [3, 31, 36, 66, 68]

seem, scheinen *shin'-en*

select *v.,* wählen *vehl'-en*

selection, Auswahl (f) *ows'-vahl*

self, selbst *zelpst*

sell, verkaufen *fer-kowf'-en* [63]

send, senden, schicken *zend'-en, shik'-en*

sense *v.,* fühlen *feül'-en*

sensible, vernünftig *fer-neunft'-eeç*

separate *adj.,* getrennt *ge-trent'*

separate *v.,* trennen *tren'-en*

September, September (m) *zep-tem'-ber*

series, Reihe (f) *ri'-e*

serious, ernst *ernst*

servant, Diener (m), Dienerin (f) *deen'-er, deen'-er-in*

serve *v.,* dienen *deen'-en* [63]

service, Dienst (m) *deenst* **room service,** Zimmer-
bedienung (f), *tsim'-er-be-deen-oong*

service charge, Bedienungskosten (pl) *be-deen'-oongs-kost-en*

set [place], setzen, anordnen *zets'-en, ahn'-ord-nen*

seven, sieben *zeeb'-en*

seventeen, siebzehn *zeep'-tsehn*

seventh, siebente *zeeb'-ent-e*

seventy, siebzig *zeep'-tseeç*

several, mehrere, verschiedene *mehr'-er-e, fer-sheed'-e-ne*

severe, streng *shtrehng*

sew, nähen *neh'-en*

shade, Schatten (m) *shaht'-en*

shampoo, Haarwaschen (n) *hahr'-vahsh-en*

shape n., Form (f) *form*

share v., verteilen *fer-til'-en*

shark, Haifisch (m) *hi'-fish*

sharp, scharf *shahrf*

shave n., Rasieren (n) *rah-zeer'-en*

shave v., sich rasieren *ziç rah-zeer'-en*

shaving cream, Rasiercreme (f) *rah-zeer'-kreh-me*

she, sie *zee*

sheep, Schaf (n) *shahf*

sheet [of paper], Bogen (m) *bohg'-en* **bedsheet,** Laken (n), Bettuch (n) *lahk'-en, bet'-tookh*

shellfish, Schaltier (n) *shahl'-teer*

shelter, Obdach (n) *ohp'-dahkh*

sherry, Sherrywein (m) *she'-ree-vin*

shine v., putzen, scheinen, leuchten *puts'-en, shin'-en, loyçt'-en*

ship n., Schiff (n) *shif* [87, 88]

ship v., senden, verschiffen *zend'-en, fer-shif'-en* [69]

shirt, Hemd (n) *hemt* [39, 66]

shiver v., zittern *tsit'-ern*

shock n., Stoss (m) *shtohs*

shoe, Schuh (m) *shoo* [68]

shoelace, Schnürsenkel (m), Schuhband (n) *shneûr'-zehnk-el, shoo'-bahnt*

shoeshine, Schuhe putzen *shoo'-e puts'-en*

shoestore, Schuhgeschäft (n) *shoo'-ge-sheft*

shoot *v.*, schiessen *shees'-en*

shop *n.*, Laden (m), Kaufladen (m) *lahd'-en, kowf'-lahd-en*

shop: to go shopping, einkaufen gehen *in'-kowf-en geh'-en* [61]

shopping center, Einkaufszentrum (n) *in'-kowfs-tsen-troom* [101]

shore, Ufer (n), Strand (m) *oof'-er, shtrahnt*

short, kurz *kurts* [66, 68]

shorts, kurze Hose (f) *kurts'-e hohz'-e*

shoulder, Schulter (f) *shult'-er*

show *n.*, Vorstellung (f), Aufführung (f) *for'-shtel-oong, owf'-feūr-oong*

show *v.*, zeigen *tsīg'-en* [63, 95]

shower [bath], Brausebad (n) *brow'-ze-baht* [36]

shrimp, Garnele (f), Krabbe (f) *gahr-neh'-le, krahb'-e*

shut *adj.*, geschlossen *ge-shlos'-en*

shut *v.*, schliessen, zumachen *shlees'-en, tsoo'-mahkh-en*

shy, schüchtern, scheu *sheūçt'-ern, shoy*

sick, krank *krahnk* [92]

side, Seite (f) *zīt'-e*

sidewalk, Bürgersteig (m) *beūrg'-er-shtik*

sight, Aussicht (f), Anblick (m) *ows'-ziçt, ahn'-blik*

sightseeing, Besuchen von Sehenswürdigkeiten (n) *be-zookh'-en fon zeh'-ens-veūrd-eeç-kīt-en* [97]

sign *n.*, Zeichen (n), Schild (n) *tsīç'-en, shilt*

sign *v.*, unterschreiben, unterzeichnen *un-ter-shrib'-en, un-ter-tsīç'-nen* [31]

signature, Unterschrift (f) *un'-ter-shrift*

silence, Ruhe (f), Stille (f) *roo'-e, shtil'-e*

silent, still, schweigend *shtil, shvīg'-ent*

silk, Seide (f) *zīd'-e*

silly, blöd, blödsinning, albern *blöēt, blöēt'-zin-eeç, ahl'-bern*

silver, Silber (n) *zil'-ber*

similar, ähnlich *ehn'-leeç*
simple, einfach *in'-fahkh*
since, seit, seitdem *zit, zit'-dehm*
sing, singen *zing'-en*
single, ledig *lehd'-eeç*
sir, Herr (m) *her*
sister, Schwester (f) *shvest'-er* [2]
sit, sitzen, sich setzen *zits'-en, ziç zets'-en* [99]
situation, Lage (f) *lahg'-e*
six, sechs *zeks*
sixteen, sechzehn *zeç'-tsehn*
sixth, sechste *zekst'-e*
sixty, sechzig *zeç'-tseeç*
size, Grösse (f) *grões'-e* [63]
skate v., schlittschuh laufen *shlit'-shoo lowf'-en*
skates n., Schlittschuhe (m, pl) *shlit'-shoo*
ski v., schi laufen *shee lowf'-en*
skis n., schi (m, pl) *shee*
skilled, skillful, geschickt *ge-shikt'*
skin, Haut (f) *howt*
skirt, Rock (m) *rok* [66]
skull, Schädel (m) *shehd'-el*
sky, Himmel (m) *him'-el*
sleep n., Schlaf (m), Schlummer (m) *shlahf, shlum'-er*
sleep v., schlafen *shlahf'-en* [95]
sleeve, Ärmel (m) *ehrm'-el* [68]
slice n., Schnitte (f) *shnit'-e*
slice v., schneiden *shnid'-en*
slide v., gleiten *glit'-en*
slip [garment], Unterrock (m) *un'-ter-rok*
slip v., schlüpfen *shlêup'-fen*
slippers, Pantoffel (m) *pahn-tof'-el*
slippery, schlüpferig *shlêup'-fer-eeç* [75]
slow, langsam *lahng'-zahm*
slowly, langsam *lahng'-zahm* [10, 42, 44]
small, klein *klin*

smart, gescheit, klug *ge-shīt', klookh*
smell *n.*, Geruch (m) *ge-rookh'*
smell *v.*, riechen *reeç'-en*
smile *n.*, Lächeln (n) *leç'-eln*
smoke *n.*, Rauch (m) *rowkh*
smoke *v.*, rauchen *rowkh'-en* [90, 95]
smooth, glatt *glaht*
snack, Imbiss (m) *im'-bis*
snow *n.*, Schnee (m) *shneh*
snow *v.*, schneien *shnī-en* [5]
so, so, also, *zoh, ahl'-zoh* **so as**, damit *dah-mit'* **so that**, so dass, damit *zoh dahs, dah-mit'*
soap, Seife (f) *zīf'-e* [39]
social, gesellschaftlich *ge-zel'-shahft-leeç*
sock, Socke (f) *zok'-e*
soda, Sodawasser (n) *zoh'-dah-vahs-er*
soft, weich *vīç*
sold, verkauft, ausverkauft *fer-kowft', ows'-fer-kowft*
solid, fest *fest*
some, einige *īn'-ee-ge*
somehow, irgendwie *eer'-gent-vee*
someone, jemand *yeh'-mahnt*
something, etwas *et'-vahs*
sometimes, manchmal *mahnç'-mahl*
somewhere, irgendwo *eer'-gent-voh*
son, Sohn (m) *zohn* [2]
song, Lied (n), Gesang (m) *leet, ge-zahng'*
soon, bald *bahlt*
sore *adj.*, wund *vunt*
sore throat, Halsschmerzen (pl), Halsweh (n) *hahls'-shmerts-en, hahls'-veh*
sorrow, Kummer (m) *kum'-er*
sorry: to be sorry, leid tun *līt toon* **I'm sorry**, es tut mir leid *es toot meer līt*
sort, Sorte (f) *zort'-e*
soul, Seele (f) *zeh'-le*

sound *n.*, Laut (m) *lowt*

soup, Suppe (f) *zup'-e* [53]

sour, sauer *zow'-er* [51]

south, Süden (m) *zêûd'-en*

southeast, Südosten (m) *zêûd'-ost-en*

southwest, Südwesten (m) *zêûd'-vest-en*

souvenir, Andenken (n) *ahn'-dehnk-en*

space, Raum (m) *rowm*

speak, sprechen *shpreç'-en* [10, 42] **do you speak English?** sprechen Sie Englisch? *shpreç'-en zee ehng'-leesh*?

special, besonder *be-zond'-er*

specialty, Spezialität (f), Sonderausgabe (f) *shpeh-tsee-ah-lee-teht'*, *zond'-er-ows-gahb-e*

speed, Geschwindigkeit (f) *ge-shvin'-deeç-kit* [75]

spell *v.*, buchstabieren *bookh-shtah-beer'-en*

spend, ausgeben, verbringen *ows'-gehb-en, fer-breeng'-en*

spicy, scharf *shahrf*

spinach, Spinat (m) *shpee-naht'*

spine, Rückgrat (n) *rêûk'-graht*

splendid, prachtvoll, herrlich *prahkht'-fol, her'-leeç*

spoiled, verdorben *fer-dohr'-ben*

spoon, Löffel (m) *lôêf'-el* [53, 54]

spot *n.*, Fleck (m) *flek*

sprain *n.*, Verrenkung (f) *fer-rehnk'-oong*

spring [season], Frühling (m) *frêû'-leeng*

spring [water], Quelle (f) *kvel'-e*

springs [of a car], Federn (f, pl) *fehd'-ern*

square *adj.*, viereckig *feer'-ek-eeç*

square *n.*, Quadrat (n) *kvahd-raht'*

stairs, Treppe (f) *trep'-e*

stamp, Briefmarke (f) *breef'-mahrk-e*

stand *v.*, stehen *shteh'-en*

star, Stern (n) *shtern* [7]

starch, Stärke (f) *shterk'-e*

start *n.*, Anfang (m) *ahn'-fahng*

start *v.*, beginnen, anfangen *be-gin'-en, ahn'-fahng-en*

state, Staat (m) *shtaht*

stateroom, Kabine (f) *kah-bee'-ne* [88]

station, Bahnhof (m) *bahn'-hohf* [85]

statue, Standbild (n), Bildsäule (f) *shtahnt'-bilt, bilt'-zoy-le*

stay *v.,* bleiben *blib'-en* [15, 37]

steak, Beefsteak (n) *beef'-shtehk*

steal *v.,* stehlen *shtehl'-en* [14]

steel, Stahl (m) *shtahl*

steep, steil *shtil*

step, Schritt (m) *shrit*

stew, Schmorgericht (n) *shmohr'-ge-riçt*

steward, Steward (m) *shtoo'-ahrt* [88]

stiff, steif *shtif*

still [quiet], still, ruhig, *shtil, roo'-eeç*

still [yet], noch *nokh*

sting *n.,* Stich (m) *shtiç*

sting *v.,* stechen *shteç'-en*

stockings, Strümpfe *shtrêumpf'-e*

stomach, Magen (m) *mahg'-en* [93]

stone, Stein (m) *shtin*

stop *n.,* Haltestelle (f) *hahl'-te-shtel-e*

stop *v.,* anhalten, aufhören *ahn'-hahlt-en, owf'-höer-en* [5, 44, 45, 85]

store *n.,* Laden, Kaufladen (m) *lahd'-en, kowf'-lahd-en* [61, 98]

storey, Stock (m) *shtok*

storm, Sturm (m), Gewitter (n) *shtoorm, ge-vit'-er*

story, Geschichte (f) *ge-shiç'-te*

straight, gerade *ge-rah'-de*

straight ahead, geradeaus *ge-rah-de-ows'* [45]

strange, sonderbar, seltsam *zond'-er-bahr, zelt'-zahm*

stranger, Fremde (m, f) *fremd'-e*

strawberry, Erdbeere (f) *ert'-beh-re*

stream, Strom (m), Bach (n) *shtrohm, bahkh*

street, Strasse (f) *shtrahs'-e* [36, 45, 99, 100]

streetcar, Strassenbanwagen (m) *shtrahs'-en-bahn-vahg-en*
strength, Kraft (f) *krahft*
string, Schnur (f) *shnoor*
strong, stark *shtahrk*
structure, Bau (m) *bow*
student, Student (m), Studentin (f) *shtoo-dent', shtoo-dent'-in*
study v., studieren *shtoo-deer'-en*
style, Stil (m) *shteel*
suburb, Vorstadt (f), Vorort (m) *for'-shtaht, for'-ort*
succeed, Erfolg haben, gelingen *ehr-folk' hahb'-en, ge-leeng'-en*
success, Erfolg (m) *ehr-folk'*
such, solcher, solch *zolç'-er, zolç*
suddenly, plötzlich *plöets'-leeç*
suffer, leiden, erleiden *lïd'-en, ehr-lïd'-en*
sufficient, genügend *ge-neüg'-ent*
sugar, Zucker (m) *tsuk'-er* [50, 51]
suggest, vorschlagen *for'-shlahg-en*
suggestion, Vorschlag (m) *for'-shlahk*
suit, Anzug (m) *ahn'-tsook*
suitcase, Handkoffer (m) *hahnt'-kof-er* [38]
summer, Sommer (m) *zom'-er*
sun, Sonne (f) *zon'-e* [5]
sunburn, Sonnenbrand (m) *zon'-en-brahnt*
Sunday, Sonntag (m) *zon'-tahkh*
sunglasses, Sonnenbrille (f) *zon'-en-bril-e*
sunny, sonnig *zon'-eeç*
supper, Abendessen (n) *ah'-bent-es-en*
sure, sicher *ziç'-er*
surface, Oberfläche (f) *oh'-ber-fleç'-e*
surprise n., Überraschung (f) *eü-ber-rahsh'-oong*
surprise v., Überraschen *eü-ber-rahsh'-en*
suspect v., in Verdacht haben *in fer-dahkht' hahb'-en*
suspicion, Verdacht (m) *fer-dahkht'*
sweater, dicke Wolljacke (f) *dik'-e vol'-yahk-e* [6]

sweep, kehren *kehr'-en*
sweet, süss *zêûs*
swim, schwimmen *shvim'-en* [101]
swollen, geschwollen *ge-shvol'-en*

table, Tisch (m) *tish* [50, 52, 56, 88]
tablecloth, Tischtuch (n) *tish'-tookh* [55]
tailor, Schneider (m) *shnid'-er*
take, nehmen *nehm'-en* [51, 66, 69, 73]   **take off,** starten *shtahr'-ten* [90]
talk, reden *rehd'-en*
tall, hoch, hoher *hohkh, hoh'-er*
tank, Tank (m) *tahnk*
taste *n.,* Geschmack (m) *ge-shmahk'*
taste *v.,* schmecken, kosten *shmek'-en, kost'-en*
tax *n.,* Steuer (f) *shtoy'-er*
taxi, Taxe (f), Taxi (f) *tahk'-se, tahk'-see* [43]
tea, Tee (m) *teh* [52]
teach, unterrichten, lehren *un'-ter-riçt-en, lehr'-en*
teacher, Lehrer (m), Lehrerin (f) *lehr'-er, lehr'-er-in*
tear [drop], Träne (f) *treh'-ne*
tear *v.,* reissen *ris'-en*
teaspoon, Teelöffel (m) *teh'-lôêf-el*
teeth, Zähne *tsehn'-e*
telegram, Telegramm (n) *teh-leh-grahm'*
telephone, Fernsprecher (m), Telefon (n) *fern'-shpreç-er, teh-leh-fohn'* [40]
telephone booth, Telefonzelle (f) *teh-leh-fohn'-tsel-e*
telephone operator, Telefonistin (f) *teh-leh-fohn-eest'-in*
television, Fernsehen (n) *fern'-zeh-en*
tell, sagen, erzählen *zahg'en, ehr-tsehl'-en* [45]
temperature, Temperatur (f) *tem-pe-ra-toor'*
temple, Tempel (m) *tem'-pel*
ten, zehn *tsehn*
tent, Zelt (n) *tselt*
tenth, zehnte *tsehnt'-e*

test, Prüfung (f) *preūf'-oong*

than, als *ahlss*

thank, danken *dahnk'-en* [101] **thank you!** danke schön!
dahnk'-e shōen!

thankful, dankbar *dahnk'-bahr*

that *adj.,* jener *yehn'-er*

that *conj.,* dass *dahs*

that *pron.,* jener *yehn'-er*

the, der, die, das *dehr, dee, dahs*

theater, Theater (n) *teh-ah'-ter* [100]

theft, Diebstahl (m) *deep'-shtahl*

their, ihr *eer*

theirs, der Ihre *dehr eer'-e*

them, sei *zee* **to them,** ihnen *ee'-nen*

then, dann, damals *dahn, dah'-mahls*

there *adv.,* dort, da *dort, dah*

therefore, deshalb *des'-hahlp*

thermometer, Fiebermesser (m), Thermometer (n) *feeb'-
er-mes-er, ter-moh-meht'-er*

these *adj. & pron.,* diese *deez'-e*

they, sie *zee*

thick, dick, dicht *dik, diçt*

thigh, Schenkel (m) *shehnk'-el*

thin, dünn, mager *dēun, mahg'-er*

thing, Sache (f), Ding (n) *zahkh'-e, deeng*

think, denken *dehnk'-en*

third, dritte *drit'-e*

thirst, Durst (m) *durst*

thirsty, durstig *durst'-eeç* [47, 48]

thirteen, dreizehn *drī'-tsehn*

thirty, dreissig *dris'-eeç*

this *adj. & pron.,* dieser *deez'-er*

those *adj. & pron.,* jene, die *yehn'-e, dee*

thoroughfare, Hauptverkehrsstrasse (f) *howpt'-fer-kehrs-
shtrahs-e*

thousand, tausend *tow'-zent*

thread, Faden (m) *fahd'-en* [69]

three, drei *dri*

throat, Kehle (f), Schlund (m) *kehl'-e, shlunt*

through *prep.,* durch *doorç*

through [finished], aus, fertig *ows, fert'-eeç*

throw, werfen *verf'-en*

thumb, Daumen (m) *dowm'-en*

thunder, Donner (m) *don'-er* [6]

Thursday, Donnerstag (m) *don'-ers-tahkh*

ticket, Fahrkarte (f), Eintrittskarte (f) *fahr'-kahrt-e, in'-trits-kahrt-e* [84, 86, 90]

ticket office, Fahrkartenschalter (m) *fahr'-kahrt-en-shahlt-er* [84]

tie [bind], binden *bind'-en*

tight, eng, knapp *ehng, knahp* [68]

tighten, anziehen *ahn'-tsee-en*

time, Zeit (f), Mal (n) *tsīt, mahl* **what time is it?** wieviel Uhr ist es? *vee-feel' oor ist es?* **on time,** zur Zeit *tsoor tsīt*

timetable, Fahrplan (m) *fahr-plahn* [84]

tip [money], Trinkgeld (n) *treenk'-gelt* [56]

tire [of a car], Reifen (m) *rīf'-en* [74]

tire *v.,* ermüden *ehr-mēūd'-en*

tired, müde *mēūd'-e* [99]

to, zu, nach *tsoo, nahkh*

toast, geröstetes Brot (n) *ge-rōēs'-te-tes broht*

tobacco, Tabak (m) *tah-bahk'* [33]

tobacconist, Tabakhändler (m) *tah-bahk'-hent-ler*

today, heute *hoy'-te* [4, 98]

toe, Zehe (f) *tseh'-e*

together, zusammen *tsoo-zahm'-en*

toilet, Toilette (f), Klosett (n), Abort (m) *toy-let'-e, kloh-zet', ahp'-ort*

toilet paper, Klosettpapier (n) *kloh-zet'-pah-peer*

tomato, Tomate (f) *toh-mah-te*

tomorrow, morgen *mor'-gen* [3, 5, 39, 95]

tongue, Zunge (f) *tsung'-e* [95]
tonight, heute abend *hoy'-te ah'-bent*
tonsils, Mandel (f) *mahnd'-el*
too [excessive], zu *tsoo*; [also], auch *owkh*
tooth, Zahn (m) *tsahn*
toothache, Zahnschmerzen (pl), Zahnweh (n) *tsahn'-shmerts-en, tsahn'-veh*
toothbrush, Zahnbürste (f) *tsahn'-béûrst-e*
toothpaste, Zahnpasta (f) *tsahn'-pahs-tah*
top [summit], Gipfel (m) *gipf'-el*
torn, zerrissen *tser-ris'-en*
total n., Gesamtbetrag (m) *ge-zahmt'-be-trahk*
touch v., berühren, anrühren *be-reûr'-en, ahn'-reûr-en*
tough, zäh *tseh*
tour, Rundreise (f), Rundfahrt (f) *runt'-riz-e, runt'-fahrt* [98, 101]
tow, schleppen *shlep'-en*
toward, zu, zum (m), zur (f), nach *tsoo, tsum, tsoor, nahkh*
towel, Handtuch (n) *hahnt'-tookh* [39]
town, Stadt (f) *shtaht*
toy, Spielzeug (n) *shpeel'-tsoyk*
toy shop, Spielzeuggeschäft (n) *shpeel'-tsoyk-ge-sheft*
traffic, Verkehr (m) *fer-kehr'*
train n., Zug (m) *tsook* [14, 83, 84, 85, 86]
transfer v., übertragen, umsteigen *eû'-ber-trahg-en, um'-shtig-en* [46]
translate v., übersetzen *eû-ber-zets'-en*
translation, Übersetzung (f) *eû'-ber-zets'-oong*
translator, Übersetzer (m) *eû-ber-zets'-er*
transmission, Getriebe (n) *ge-treeb'-e*
transportation, Beförderung (f) *be-föer'-der-oong*
travel v., reisen *riz'-en*
traveler, Reisende (m, f) *riz'-end-e*
traveler's check, Reisescheck (m) *riz'-e-shek* [30]
tray, Tablett (n), Servierbrett (n) *tahb-let', ser-veer'-bret*
tree, Baum (m) *bowm*

trip, Fahrt (f), Reise (f) *fahrt, rīz'-e* [89]
trousers, Hosen (f, pl) *hohz'-en*
truck, Lastwagen (m) *lahst'-vahg-en*
true, wahr *vahr*
trunk, Koffer (m) *kof'-er*
truth, Wahrheit (f) *vahr'-hīt*
try *v.,* versuchen *fer-zookh'-en* **try on,** anprobieren *ahn'-proh-beer-en* [63, 68]
Tuesday, Dienstag *deens'-tahkh*
turn *n.,* Wendung (f) *vend'-oong*
turn *v.,* drehen, sich umdrehen, umwenden, einbeigen *dreh'-en, ziç um'-dreh-en, um'-vend-en, in'-beeg-en* [45]
twelve, zwölf *tsvöelf*
twenty, zwanzig *tsvahnts'-eeç*
twice, zweimal *tsvī'-mahl*
twin beds, Doppelbetten *dop'-el-bet-en*
two, zwei *tsvī*

ugly, hässlich *hes'-leeç*
umbrella, Regenschirm (m) *rehg'-en-sheerm* [6]
uncle, Onkel (m) *onk'-el*
uncomfortable, unbequem *un'-be-kvehm*
unconscious, bewusstlos *be-vust'-lohs*
under *prep.,* unter *un'-ter*
underneath *prep.,* unter *un'-ter*
undershirt, Unterhemd (n) *un'-ter-hemt*
understand, verstehen *fer-shteh'-en* [10]
underwear, Unterwäsche (f), Unterzeug (n) *un'-ter-vesh-e, un'-ter-tsoyk*
undress *v.,* sich ausziehen *ziç ows'-tsee-en*
unequal, ungleich *un'-glīç*
unfair, ungerecht *un'-ge-reçt*
unfortunate, unglücklich *un'-glöük-leeç*
unhappy, unglücklich *un'-glöük-leeç*
unhealthy, ungesund *un'-ge-zunt*

United States, die Vereinigten Staaten (pl) *dee fer-in'-eeçt-en shtaht'-en*
university, Universität (f) *oo-nee-ver-see-teht'*
unless, es sei denn, wenn nicht *es zi den, wen niçt*
unlucky, unglücklich *un'-gleûk-leeç*
unpack, auspacken *ows'-pahk-en*
unpleasant, unangenehm *un'-ahn-ge-nehm*
unsafe, unsicher *un'-ziç-er*
until, bis *bis*
untrue, unwahr, falsch *un'-vahr, fahlsh*
unusual, ungewöhnlich *un'-ge-vōēn-leeç*
up, auf, oben *owf, oh'-ben*
upper, ober *oh'-ber*
upstairs, oben *oh'-ben*
urgent, dringend *dreeng'-ent*
us, uns *uns*
use *n.*, Gebrauch (m) *ge-browkh'* [33]
use *v.*, gebrauchen, benutzen *ge-browkh'-en, be-nuts'-en*
useful, nützlich, brauchbar *neûts'-leeç, browkh'-bahr*
useless, nutzlos, unbrauchbar *nuts'-lohs, un'-browkh-bahr*
usual, gewöhnlich *ge-vōēn'-leeç*

vacant, frei, leer *frī, lehr*
vacation, Ferien (pl) *feh'-ree-en*
vaccination, Impfung (f) *impf'-oong*
valuable, wertvoll *vert'-fol*
value *n.*, Wert (m) *vert*
vanilla, Vanille (f) *vah-neel'-ye*
variety, Verschiedenheit (f) *fer-sheed'-en-hit*
veal, Kalbfleisch (n) *kahlp'-flīsh*
vegetables, Gemüse (n) *ge-meûz'-e*
very, sehr *zehr*
vest, Weste (f) *vest'-e*
victim, Opfer (n) *opf'-er*
view *n.*, Aussicht (f) *ows'-ziçt* [36]

village, Dorf (n) *dorf*
vinegar, Essig (m) *es'-eeç*
visa *n.,* Visum (n) *veez'-oom*
visit *n.,* Besuch (m) *be-zookh'* [98, 100]
visit *v.,* besuchen *be-zookh'-en*
voice, Stimme (f) *shtim'-e*
voyage *n.,* Seereise (f) *zeh'-riz-e*

waist, Taille (f) *tahl'-ye*
wait *v.,* warten *vahrt-en* [11, 12, 44]
waiter, Kellner (m) *kel'-ner* [50, 55]
waiting room, Wartesaal (m) *vahrt'-e-zahl* [86]
waitress, Kellnerin (f), Fräulein (n) *kel'-ner-in, froy'-lin*
   [50]
wake up, wecken *vek'-en* [39]
walk *n.,* Spaziergang (m) *shpah-tseer'-gahng*
walk *v.,* gehen *geh'-en*
wall, Wand (f), Mauer (f) *vahnt, mow'-er*
wallet, Geldbeutel (m) *gelt'-boyt-el*
want *v.,* wollen *vol'-en*   **I want,** ich will *iç vil*
warm, warm *vahrm* [4, 6, 51, 55]
warn, warnen *vahrn'-en*
warning, Warnung (f) *vahrn'-oong*
wash *v.,* waschen *vahsh'-en* [39, 74]
wasp, Wespe (f) *vesp'-e*
watch *n.,* Armbanduhr (f) *ahrm'-bahnt-oor*
watch *v.,* beobachten, bewachen *beh-oh-bahkht'-en, be-*
   vahkh'-en
water, Wasser (n) *vahs'-er* [6, 50, 73, 100]
waterfall, Wasserfall (m) *vahs'-er-fahl*
wave [ocean], Welle (f) *vel'-e*
way [manner], Weise (f) *viz'-e*
we, vir *veer*
weak, schwach *shvahkh*
wear *v.,* tragen *trahg'-en*
weather, Wetter (n) *vet'-er* [4, 6]

Wednesday, Mittwoch (m) *mit'-vokh*

week, Woche (f) *vokh'-e* [37]

weigh, wiegen *veeg'-en*

weight, Gewicht (n) *ge-viçt'*

welcome *n.,* Empfang (m), Willkommen (n) *emp-fahng', vil'-kom-en*

well, gut, wohl *goot, vohl* **well done** [food], gut durchgebraten *goot doorç'-ge-braht-en*

well [for water] Brunnen (m) *brun'-en*

west, Westen (m) *vest'-en*

wet, nass *nahs* [75]

what, was *vahs* **what else?** was noch? *vahs nokh?*

wheel, Rad (n) *raht*

when, wenn, wann *ven, vahn*

whenever, so oft *zoh oft*

where, wo *voh* **where is . . . ?** wo ist . . . ? *voh ist . . . ?* **where are . . . ?** wo sind . . . ? *voh zint . . . ?*

wherever, wo immer *voh im'-er*

which, welcher, welches *velç'-er, velç'-es*

while, während, indem *veh'-rent, in-dehm'*

whip *n.,* Peitsche (f) *pitch'-e*

white, weiss *vis*

who, wer *vehr*

who (rel.), der, die, das *dehr, dee, dahs*

whole, ganz *gahnts*

whom, wen *vehn*

whose? wessen? *ves'-en*

why, warum *vah-room'*

wide, breit *brit* [68, 75]

width, Breite (f), Weite (f) *brit'-e, vit'-e*

wife, Frau (f), Gattin (f) *frow, gaht'-in* [2]

wild, wild *vilt*

willing, bereitwillig sein *be-rit'-vil-iç zin*

win *v.,* gewinnen *ge-vin'-en*

wind, Wind (m) *vint* [7]

window, Fenster (n) *fens'-ter* [38, 85]

windshield, Windschutzscheibe (f) *vint'-shuts-shīb-e* [78]
wine, Wein (m) *vīn* **red wine,** Rotwein (m) *roht'-vīn*
  white wine, Weisswein (m) *vīs'-vīn*
wing, Flügel (m) *flēū̄g'-el*
winter, Winter (m) *vin'-ter*
wipe, wischen *vish'-en* [78]
wise, weise, klug *vīz'-e, klookh*
wish *n.,* Wunsch (m) *vunsh*
wish *v.,* wünschen *vēūnsh'-en* [44, 63] **I wish,** ich
  wünsche *iç vēūnsh'-e*
with, mit *mit*
without, ohne *oh'-ne*
woman, Frau (f), Weib (n) *frow, vīp* [9]
wonderful, wunderbar *vund'-er-bahr*
wood, Holz (n) *holts*
woods, Wald (m) *vahlt*
wool, Wolle (f) *vol'-e*
word, Wort (n) *vort*
work *n.,* Arbeit (f) *ahr'-bīt*
work *v.,* arbeiten *ahr'-bīt-en*
world, Welt (f) *velt*
worried, besorgt *be-zorkt'*
worse, schlechter, schlimmer *shleçt-er, shlim'-er*
worth, Wert (m) *vert*
wound [injury], Wunde (f) *vund'-e*
wrap *v.,* einpacken, einwickeln *in'-pahk-en, in'-vik-eln* [69]
wrist, Handgelenk (n) *hahnt'-ge-lehnk*
wristwatch, Armbanduhr (f) *ahrm'-bahnt-oor*
write, schreiben *shrīb'-en* [29]
writing, Schriftstück (n) *shrift'-shtēū̄k*
wrong, falsch, unrecht *fahlsh, unt'-reçt* [12]

x ray, Röntgenstrahlen (pl) *rōent'-gen-shtrahl-en*

yard, Hof (m) *hohf*
year, Jahr (n) *yahr* [90]

yellow, gelb *gelp*
yes, ja, doch *yah, dokh*
yesterday, gestern *gest'-ern* [5]
yet, noch *nokh*
you, Sie, du, ihr *zee, doo, eer*
young, jung *yung*
your, Ihr, dein, euer *eer, din, oy'-er*
yours, der (die, das) Ihre, Deine, Euere *dehr (dee, dahs) eer'-e, din'-e, oy'-er-e*

zero, Null (f) *nul*
zipper, Reissverschluss (m) *ris'-fer-shlus*

CONVERSION TABLES

Length
1 centimeter (cm) .. 0.39 inch
1 meter (m) = 39.36 inches
1 kilometer (km) = 0.62 mile
1 inch = 2.54 cm.
1 foot = 0.30 m.
1 mile = 1.61 km.

Weight
1 gramm (gm) = 0.04 ounce
1 kilo (kg) = 2.20 pounds
1 ounce = 28.35 gm.
1 pound = 453.59 gm.

Volume
1 liter = 0.91 dry quart
1 liter = 1.06 liquid quarts
1 pint liquid = 0.47 liter
1 US quart liquid = 0.95 liter
1 US gallon = 3.78 liters

Temperature

Celsius (°C):	−17.8	0	10	20	30	37	37.8	100
Fahrenheit (°F):	0	32	50	68	86	98.6	100	212

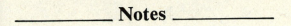

_____ **Notes** _____

Notes

Notes

Notes

Notes